THE
GIFT of
THE DEER

Also by

Helen Hoover

A PLACE IN THE WOODS
THE LONG-SHADOWED FOREST
THE YEARS OF THE FOREST

Books For Young Readers:

ANIMALS AT MY DOORSTEP
ANIMALS NEAR AND FAR
GREAT WOLF AND THE GOOD WOODSMAN

THE
GIFT *of*
THE
DEER

by Helen Hoover

pen-and-ink drawings from life
by Adrian Hoover

Houghton Mifflin Company   Boston

Library of Congress Cataloging in Publication Data

Hoover, Helen.
  The gift of the deer.

  Reprint of the 1979 ed. published by Knopf,
New York.
  1. White-tailed deer—Legends and stories.
I. Title.
QL795.D3H6 1981   599.73'57   80-25471
ISBN 0-395-30534-9 (pbk.)

Printed in the United States of America

Q 10 9 8 7 6 5 4 3 2 1

Reprinted by arrangement with Alfred A. Knopf, Inc.

Houghton Mifflin Company paperback 1981

Portions of this book have appeared in the January 1966, February 1966, and March 1966 issues of *Woman's Journal*, London.

This book is for

CLAIRE GOMERSALL,

who always believed in it

Contents

ACKNOWLEDGMENTS

My sincere thanks go to Dr. T. D. Nicholson, Chair-
man, The American Museum—Hayden Planetarium,
for suggestions which helped my husband prepare
his drawing of the heavens; to Dr. John C. Schlotthauer, College of Veterinary Medicine, Department
of Veterinary Pathology and Parasitology, University of Minnesota, for correcting my paragraphs on
deer disease; to Milton H. Stenlund, Game Manager,
Minnesota Department of Conservation, for his
estimate of the Minnesota timber-wolf population;
to James W. Kimball, staff writer, Minneapolis *Star
& Tribune*, for ideas stirred by his column; to the
editors of *Audubon* and *Defenders of Wildlife News*
for permission to adapt material which first appeared
in these magazines; to Angus Cameron for his
editorial advice; and to my husband, who not only
labored mightily on the illustrations but also read
and reread the growing manuscript, adding to it
from his store of memories.

the
first
year

PETER

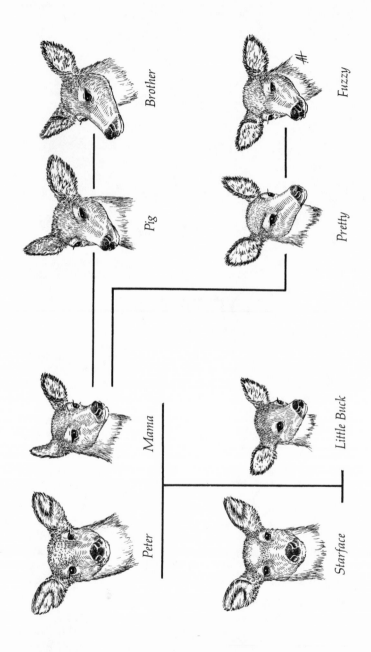

December 25

Some fifteen feet from the door of the two-room log cabin where my husband and I have lived every winter and some summers of the past eleven years there is a white cedar tree, one of many in the ancient forest that surrounds the cabin. This tree, seriously damaged by years of scanty rainfall, is dying. Near its roots lies a little pile of branches whose bare, dry twigs give perching space to small birds and cover to timid deer mice and voles. Neither Ade nor I will ever move the branches or fell the tree, even after it is dead, for this was Peter Whitetail's tree and the stripped branches are all that remain of green and fragrant cedar cut for him on the memorable day that brought him to our clearing.

Peter was a buck who came to us, not as a fawn but in the fullness of his maturity. To have the trust of any deer is a joy, but when a buck, reserved and cautious as these regal animals are, accepts you as a friendly benefactor it is a very special thing. And Peter was a special kind of buck —gentle, generous, great of heart.

So, on a Christmas Day, in the kitchen of our summer cabin . . .

I popped a length of split birch into the purring range, saw that its somewhat doubtful oven thermometer still indicated a proper temperature for turkey roasting, and took the coffee pot from its place on the ring of iron warming trivets that surrounded the stove pipe. As I settled down in the low walnut rocker with my black coffee, I decided that the kitchen would have pleased my Great-aunt Anne, who died in 1932 at the age of ninety-four. The walnut pie safe with sides perforated in patterns, the dry sink with its washpan and dishpan, the oil lamps waiting for the dusk—even the fragrance of wood smoke belonged to her era. My plaid wool shirt and heavy leather boots would have pleased her because they are practical, but my woodsman's pants would have "shocked her modesty" and brought on a tight-lipped silence. However, if she and Uncle John had lived where Ade and I do, forty-five miles from a village on a one-way road, with our nearest neighbor miles away through the vastness of the northern forest, she would have worn pants—and the devil take her critics. Smiling at her memory, I glanced at the clock, a modern alarm which impressed me momentarily as a time traveler in the old-fashioned kitchen. Two thirty, and at least another hour before the bird would be done.

I stood up, stretched, and went into the high-ceilinged living room, closed for the winter because the frame house was not insulated. The room's dead air was colder by several degrees than the twenty below zero outside, but it felt refreshing after the heat of the kitchen. The walnut Dutch cupboard and maple chairs looked as inhospitable as their counterparts in some museum display room, but glittering frost granules powdered the varicolored stones of the fireplace and icy feathers turned the small-paned windows into luminous miracles of geometric design. I wondered who first owned the furniture and if their ladies had held hand-screens of Berlin work to protect their delicate faces from the heat of other, older fireplaces.

The chill from my own fireplace stones brought me back to the present, and I jumped for the kitchen door. Christmas is for dreaming, but not at the expense of letting the cooking fire go out, especially when we were expecting Jacques Plessis for dinner at four o'clock. Jacques's name, pronounced in the French fashion, always sends my summer visitors into ecstatic fantasies of bateaux full of furs and voyageurs, their paddles sweeping through the waters of the border lake that separates our Minnesota shore from Canada, moving down the Voyageurs Highway to the rhythmic chant of "Alouette." Actually, Jacques is American-born of parents of French descent and I am sure has never said "By gar!" in his life. He is an old-time lumberjack, slow and quiet of speech, with the size and strength of these now almost legendary men, and an appetite developed in the days when trees were cut with handsaws. Jacques would lean back in his chair and politely starve if dinner were late.

I knelt by the big oven and poked the bird with a fork. It was time to remove its cloth covering and let it brown. I thought wistfully of the foil I had forgotten to have mailed to us from town, then soothed myself by recalling that Great-aunt Anne had done very well without such luxuries. The turkey would be done on time. I wondered how Ade, a hundred yards away in the winter log cabin, was getting on with his voluntary job of peeling the potatoes and grinding the carrots for salad. I was meditating on the importance of cooperation in small things as well as in large if two people are to live happily in as nearly complete isolation as Ade and I when I heard branches snapping in the woods, loud as little firecrackers in that stillness. I stepped outside.

The sun, below the tops of the great spruces, reached pale fingers between the trees to draw their shadows long and blue across the little clearing. Last night's snow, wind-rippled on the ground and weighing down the branches, sparkled like chips from a star. Here and there clumps of snow slid from their precarious support of needles, separated, and drifted away like steam. Under the blue of the sky, opalescent with falling frost, the silence waited—until branches snapped again. I tried to look into the leafless maple brush that covered the hill between the house and the little side road. Did one shadow move among others in the thicket? Probably not. The temperature was beginning to drop as evening approached, and trees and branches pop and crack as their freezing increases.

The heat from the stove was melting the snow on the kitchen's slanting roof and icicles dripped as they formed on the eaves. Two chickadees, puffed into black-and-white feather balls, flew down to hang upside down on the edge of the shingles and drink from the unseasonable drops of water. Some blue jays squawked in the treetops and I scattered cracked corn on the snow, then went inside to watch them drift down to eat. Suddenly they flew away, startled by the voices I heard from the woods.

I opened the door as Jacques and Ade stomped from the edge of the trees, beating the snow into a wider path and puffing clouds of frosty breath ahead of them. Jacques peered over a heaped-up double armload of stove wood and Ade dragged a toboggan, on which was the oval shape of a burlap-wrapped platter, a large sheet of plywood, a black iron spider, and three pails. All I needed was a Paisley shawl and a long, full skirt to turn the scene into something by Currier and Ives.

Amid shouts of "Merry Christmas" and "How's the turkey?" the latter even more enthusiastic than the former, we crowded inside. Ear-flapped caps and heavy gloves flew here and there and I pointed to the stove and said: "Ten minutes." Ade began to unwrap the platter and Jacques leaned against the pie safe. Tall, broad, bronzed, and heavy, he filled the kitchen. Ade, who is slim and wiry, once said that when he stands beside Jacques he probably gives the impression of a side view.

"I thought you were cutting timber to keep your figure," I said to Jacques, "but you look as if you've gained."

Smiling, and with the air of an indulgent uncle, he removed from his mackinaw a box of chocolate-covered cherries and the largest buttercup squash I ever saw.

I was so tickled that I sat crooning over the squash. We had no car in those days and brought staple foods by boat down the lake. When it froze over, supplies had to be gotten by mail and had to be carried in Ade's packsack for the last three miles along the side road. Store candy was excess baggage and fresh things were out. Even a squash would freeze after an hour at thirty below.

Beaming because his presents were a success, Jacques, who likes to know everything but who is too polite to ask questions, said casually: "I was surprised to see smoke over here as I came along the road. Didn't know you used this house in winter."

I pulled the turkey in its pan out onto the open oven door.

"Take a look at this brute. I asked for a big one, and when this twenty-six-pound bird came it wouldn't go into the oven next door. By pure luck we kept this range. We'd have gotten rid of it if there'd been any way to move it up the hill. I've been very cozy while cooking. Thirty-five degrees on the floor and ninety-seven at head height. The bird is done—if anybody cares."

While Ade and Jacques maneuvered the turkey onto the platter, I set out flour and seasoning for gravy. Jacques, pouring drippings into the iron spider, said tentatively: "Nice you had a pan to hold it."

Ade laughed. "As you can plainly see, that is a piece of galvanized sheet iron, dug out of the snow, cleaned with gasoline, scrubbed with a brush, and cut and bent to fit both bird and oven. You will note that I made a nice little pouring spout at one corner."

I tipped the gravy into a kettle and covered it. Jacques smothered the fire with ashes to safely smolder out. Ade slid the turkey platter onto the plywood. A few moments later we marched through the woods, Ade carrying the turkey triumphantly, I stumbling in his too widely spaced footsteps with the gravy in one hand and a book I had not opened in the other, and Jacques, behind me, candy and squash again under his jacket, hauling the toboggan on which the pails of unbreakables bounced and clattered.

Rough-barked pine boles, standing apart from us with the dignity of their two centuries, spread their lowest branches fifty feet above our heads. The dense boughs of balsam fir and spruce shut out the sky, and their seedlings stood beside the path, living Christmas trees. The light was pale and diffuse, scattered from the minute crystal facets of the snow. And from all around wild dark eyes watched, wary and hidden, the watchers ready to fly or run if we should prove hostile as well as strange. But one watcher knew us and had no compunctions about approaching. From the top of a spruce a gray jay glided on spread wings, lit on the plywood, snatched a loose flap of lusciously oily turkey skin, and flashed away.

An hour later, when half the turkey was a handsome ruin, we sat around the drop-leaf table in the log-cabin living room and considered whether any more mashed potatoes, sweet potatoes, beets, peas, cranberries, raw carrot salad, watermelon-rind pickles, Anadama bread, or chocolate-coconut pie could safely be consumed. I was as stuffed as the turkey had been, and I still dreamed of the past.

The snug cabin, with its hand-hewn round-log walls and beams and ridgepoles, whispered of an era earlier than Great-aunt Anne's, of the home earlier forebears might have built in the days of George II, after they had left their island home to cross the wild Atlantic and settle in the wooded colony of Virginia.

The Christmas tree in the corner, most of its paper

needles gone, was decorated with silvery aluminum icicles and real pine cones. On one of its branches was a broken glass trumpet, still with a touch of gilt and green, which, along with the tree and me, was experiencing its forty-eighth Christmas. It took me back to Christmases in the Victorian house where I was born.

On the morning of this important day the heavy oak sliding doors that separated the back drawing room from the front parlor were always tight shut until Father, Mother, and I—running ahead of them with my Mary Pickford curls flopping—came home from church. After wraps were hung up with agonizing slowness, we took our places in the drawing room, Father at the left door, Mother at the right, and I standing where I could look through as soon as the slightest crack appeared. After another wait, to increase the suspense of the big moment I suppose, they grasped the doors and pulled. As often as not, Father's door jumped off its rollers and while he muttered and yanked and Mother murmured "Tom! The baby!" I danced from one foot to the other until the doors were opened, not with a flourish but by main strength.

The little artificial tree, centered before the wide front window, stood on the tall pedestal that usually held Mother's fern, whose six-foot fronds trailed to the floor from a hand-painted jardiniere. Furry ropes of golden tinsel were draped round and round the tree, delicate glass ornaments quivered on its branches, and white-wicked candles waited in green-painted metal brackets, snapped onto the branch tips by clamps like clothespins. While Father lighted them, so tense with being careful that his moustache seemed more bristly than ever, Mother, chin uplifted by the choker collar of her shirtwaist, stood in front of the upright piano with a bucket of water ready. There was one glorious occasion when a branch *did* catch fire and Mother extinguished both fire and Father with one splash.

In spite of the years between, the sense of anticipation still clung to me on this Christmas Day, perhaps because the dinner and the three contented people were timeless.

And so was the small span of virgin timber, somehow spared by both fire and the axes of the lumbermen at the turn of the century, that lay between our cabins. I went to the window and looked up, up, up at a white pine on the forest's edge, twenty feet away across a tiny garden plot. A sapling when the Declaration of Independence was signed, it now stood aloof as though wrapped in its memories. I wondered how I could be so petty as to still feel something like disappointment because my adult Christmas did not hold the special thrill I had known as a child.

Again I heard branches snap, this time very near, and my surprise stepped out of the forest into the clearing— a deer.

He headed straight for some Swiss-chard seed stalks that protruded above the snow in the garden and began to eat. He did not even seem aware of the house. His coat was ruffled and he was so thin that every rib stood out and I could see the bones in his flanks. His legs trembled as he stood and his head shook as he pulled the seed stalks loose. I made gestures to Jacques, who had known deer from boyhood. As he and Ade came quietly to stand, one on each side of me, the buck looked up at us. His face was gaunt and its fur pitted. His right ear was raggedly notched and his eyes were dull. He jerked as though to run away, then dropped his head again to the seeds.

Jacques gave his special grunt of suppressed fury.

"Some damfool's taken a pop at him and hit his head with fine shot," he snapped. "Look at his left eye—it's blind. Happened maybe two months ago in the grouse season. It'd take him that long to get so poor. Look at him! He's near starved. Wouldn't come this close to a house and people otherwise. No wild buck would." His voice subsided to a muffled growl. "Maybe he'd be better off if they'd killed him."

"No," I said, following his unspoken thought. "No! Can we feed him?"

"You can try. He's still on his feet. He'll look for more, now that he's found those seeds. Let him snoop 'round the place and see you in the windows. Don't make any sudden moves to startle him. Then give him cedar. Ade can cut some of those branches the poor critter can smell but can't reach. Cedar'll help deer when they're so far gone they can't stand up. I've hauled 'em out of the woods and put 'em in a shed. When they're starved they eat all kinds of stuff they can't digest—dead twigs, sticks, anything. Gives 'em compaction."

"What's that?" Ade asked.

"Stuff wads up in their first stomach—we used to call it compaction in the old days. Anyway, once I'd get one of 'em in the shed, I'd put cedar in with him. If he was too far gone to eat it, I'd shoot him and put him out of his misery, but if he could nibble, he'd get well. I'd know when he was ready to go because he'd try to kick and butt the shed walls down. I'd open the door and duck to one side and

out he'd come—full of ginger again, leapin' off into the woods with his flag flyin' high. Made me feel mighty good." He looked sideways at me. "If he fattens up he'll be a mighty big pet—around two fifty pounds. Sure you won't be afraid of him?"

I stared. "Heavens, no. With us the only people within miles, it's almost miraculous that he managed to stumble in here. He won't bother us. Maybe I'm superstitious—but I'd bet on it."

"I wouldn't take you. Funny—animals know when you don't mean 'em any harm. They can smell when you're scared or mad, but they can't tell the difference. Queer, that."

"Not so queer," I said. "Fear and anger both send adrenalin into your system and make you sweat. Maybe that's what they smell."

The buck had nosed his way to the near side of the garden, only six feet from the window. He looked up, but this time he did not start, just dropped his head again and went on with his search for food.

"That old tree pruner will be fine for cutting cedar," Ade said.

"Peter is a nice name," Jacques suggested.

"Yes. Peter Whitetail," Ade agreed.

Peter having been named and his future hopefully planned, we set about watching him, first from one window, then another.

With painstaking care he nosed every hummock and hollow in the garden but found only a few edible frozen stalks. He chewed some dead raspberry canes and a small dry shoot of red-berried elder. He snatched eagerly at a spindly asparagus stalk and at length moved to the front of the house, where he painfully tried to rise on his shaking hind legs to reach the green cedar branches a few inches above his head. Unable to lift himself, he stood panting for several minutes, then sniffed the bleached bones of a turkey carcass, nailed onto a cedar trunk at Thanksgiving as a source of calcium and phosphorus for the squirrels. Chewing desperately and pitifully, he finally wrenched the bones loose from the tree and crunched and swallowed most of the thinner bits. He raised his head, followed the scent of suet to a wire-mesh feeder hung on a branch for the birds. It was level with the top of his head and, in a sort of tottering lunge, he managed to rear a little and knock it to the ground with his nose. He pawed at it and stamped on it, tried futilely to bite through the wire. Then he reached his head down and licked at the fat through the mesh.

Jacques reached for his jacket, warming on a chairback near the stove.

"I'd better hustle. Don't want everybody to be abed in case I get stalled on the way home. And the sooner I go, the sooner you can try to help that poor critter. He'll run when I go out, but not far, and that suet'll bring him back."

"I'll go up to the road with you," Ade said, turning down the fur-lined earflaps of his cap. "You can use some help getting started and I'll take the pruner and cut some branches on the way back."

With the wrapped remains of the pie in his hand, Jacques looked at Peter, still licking the suet cage.

"Tomorrow take him out anything you can spare—potato skins, bread maybe. Deer don't usually eat meat, but this guy sure goes for suet. Salt, too. He'll come for what you give him and be your friend as long as he lives."

With a last "Merry Christmas," Jacques opened the door slowly and stepped out. Peter started and looked fixedly at him. With his front hoofs on the suet cage, he stood firm until Ade, too, appeared outside. Then he whirled and tried to run, but staggered and almost fell. Glancing fearfully back with his good eye, he walked into the brush as fast as he could.

While Ade was helping build and control a small fire under the pan of Jacques's truck to warm the oil so that it would flow, I lighted the lamps and considered food for Peter. As a starter I took the wrapped potato peelings from the sheet-iron airtight stove we use for a trash and garbage burner as well as an auxiliary heater. I could steal a little from our canned vegetables. There were ten pounds of suet in the fifty-five-gallon oil drum that stands on the shaded north side of the cabin and serves as our winter freezer. The birds would not miss small rations for Peter, and they should be very small at first. Too much fat on a starved digestive system not designed for meat might be harmful.

I dug out some suet and knelt on the snow, struggling to close the bolt-and-spring contraption that Ade had designed to prevent fishers, those latch-lifting big cousins of the weasels, from raiding our meat supply in the drum. I heard Jacques's engine start, the clank of the truck's tailgate as it went over a snow ridge in the road, then the snap-snap of the pruner. Ade, so loaded with branches that he looked like a walking tree, skidded and slid down the path and laid the rich-scented greenery appropriately under our largest white cedar, near the door but somewhat secluded by smaller cedars, maple brush, and the miniature house and run that sheltered Bedelia, our pet black hen.

The early dusk had darkened into night before Ade and I finished clearing away the remains of our feast. We waited a long time by the window in the darkened kitchen, while aurora light flickered and flared green in the sky, but Peter did not come.

If he understood that a man had injured him, he might not dare come near the cabin again after he had seen us outside. On the other hand, if he had been far away from the shooter, as the minor nature of most of his face wounds indicated, he would not know what had happened to him. He would have experienced only a feeling of shock and pain, while darkness spread from his left side where he had seen his familiar forest before.

Only?

Suddenly I was sickened and furious at the human being who had fired such a senseless shot. At best, he was thoughtless; at worst, cruel. All over the world men were quarreling and threatening, warring and indulging in private fights, and some trigger-happy unknown had brought that reasonless brutality into our forest, where no wild animal would injure another except for food or in defense of its life or young. Because of this, Peter had wandered —confused, suffering, handicapped, starving—as he tried inadequately to adjust to the partial blindness he could not understand. I was very near tears—whether out of pity for Peter or despair at the unhappy state of mind that makes destroyers out of men, I am not sure—when Ade touched my arm and pointed up the path.

Halfway to the road, between two tree boles that looked like gateposts, Peter sniffed the slight flow of air that passed across our clearing to him. The aurora had changed from green to red, and the snow before him glowed like a carpet of rose quartz. Still sniffing, his head high and stretched forward, he began to walk down the hill, faster and faster until he was as near trotting as he could manage in his weakened condition. Straight on the scent of the cedar he came until he buried his nose in it and began to eat.

As though he read my mind, Ade said: "Things aren't quite so bad when you can help undo them, are they?"

At midnight an unusual chill in the cabin woke me and I went out to check on the weather. The thermometer had dropped to an ominous thirty-seven degrees below zero and would drop more before morning. Gusts of wind brought needles of snow from the north and in the distance I could hear the faint roar of an approaching storm. We would need a helper fire in the airtight stove in the morning. As I turned from the woodpile with my arms loaded something moving under the big cedar tree caught my eye and I directed my flashlight beam there.

Peter, who had curled up in the snow to sleep, lifted his head toward the light, then settled down again. Beside him, nibbling at the bark of a cedar stump, was a snowshoe hare. On a branch above, no doubt hoping for a mouse, a little saw-whet owl peered at the ground.

In spite of the bitter cold I watched for minutes,

amazed and marveling. There is a legend—from Norway, I think—which says that all lost animals come home at Christmastime.

Peter was no longer lost.

December 26
to February 3

In the dimness of early morning I woke to the sounds of wood crackling in the airtight stove and wind roaring in the trees. I slid out of bed, wrapped my wool robe around me, grabbed my clothes, and scooted across the cold floor to toast myself by the stove. As I dressed, Ade came down the path with two 5-gallon cans of fuel oil on the toboggan. A blast of icy air accompanied him and one of the cans inside.

"It's forty-three below," he said, pouring oil into the big space heater. "And the wind—it's almost a full gale. There isn't a sign of life outside."

As the coffee dripped, I looked out the window. The sky was a pale robin's-egg blue and perfectly clear, but visibility on the ground was cut to fifty feet by slanting veils of blowing, drifting snow. The wind lifted it in swirls, fanned it out, piled it in long, knife-edged ridges. A beautiful day, but a savage one, hard on man and beast. No wonder the birds and squirrels were staying in their shelters, waiting for the sun to rise a little higher, and perhaps for the wind to drop, before they came out to feed. Then I saw Peter.

With his head down against the wind he was making his way laboriously from the partial shelter he had found in the maple brush on the hillside. He shook as though he were palsied. He braced himself cautiously before lifting a foot to step forward, then suddenly he stumbled and went down in the snow. Slowly he gathered his legs under him, pushed up on the knees of his forelegs, straightened his hind legs, and surged fully upright. Then he rested, his nose almost touching the snow, before he again began to move slowly toward the house.

As Ade made a smothered sound of pity, I began to fix breakfast for Peter. To the potato skins I had salvaged the night before and the suet, I added leftover peas, mashed potatoes, turkey gravy, and some of the cracked corn we kept for our hen. Everything but the corn would freeze solid in minutes, but I did not think Peter would mind. If he could chew turkey ribs, he could manage mashed-potato ice, especially if I shaped the potatoes into convenient-sized lumps. I tore a big piece of corrugated paper from a box that waited to be burned in the airtight and put the food on it in separate heaps, so that he could leave any of the portions that did not appeal to him.

When I opened the door, Peter was almost within arm's reach, staring at the cabin with intense concentration. His face, so thin that the shape of his skull showed through the roughened and shot-torn fur, was covered with frost from his breath. His blind eye was frosted shut. He flinched as I stepped outside, then his nostrils quivered as he smelled the food. His breath came in heavy, straining gasps as he pushed his head forward, mouth open and pink tongue partly out. I put the food on the step and backed inside.

He was doubtful of the paper but, after carefully sniffing around its edges, cleaned it to the last crumb, licking it thoroughly as though to make sure nothing had been missed. When he looked at Ade and me through the glass of the kitchen door, his eye no longer was so dull and he held his head up with something like confidence. Then he tapped on the step with a hoof, ducked his head several times, and waited, tongue tip out.

"That's plain enough," Ade said. "He's doing his best to tell us he wants more."

"But what can I give him? Maybe a can of peas?"

"Carrots! I ground about three times too many yesterday."

Ade reached into our icebox—one of the old-fashioned kind, but without ice—and brought out a heaped dish from the bottom, which the cold from the floor chilled enough to make the space our winter vegetable keeper.

Peter ate the carrots with enthusiasm. Finished, he licked his lips, captured a small piece that adhered to his black nose, shook his ears, and turned eagerly toward the door. For the first time I realized that the slight changes of a wild animal's facial expression might, taken together with circumstances, convey meaning to a human. Unless I was greatly mistaken, Peter *liked* carrots. And I had been wondering what we would do with the bushel and a half of them we had buried in boxes of sand under Ade's drawing table—the only large crop we had taken from our garden in the thin, poor soil of the forest.

With one of the rapid changes of the northern winter, the noontime temperature was up to zero and the bitter wind had died. I was standing in the yard enjoying the dry, cold-freshened air and tracing the turquoise zigzags of shadow across the ranks of miniature snow dunes when I heard Jacques whistling as he snowshoed down Ade's toboggan track.

"What brings you back so soon?"

"Just thought I'd ask about the one-eyed jack."

While I described Peter's breakfast in detail, I took some broken graham crackers from my jacket pocket and fed the pieces to gray jays who made spectacular glides from a cedar top to my hand. ". . . so Ade ground up a quart of carrots and is across the road cutting cedar now," I finished.

Jacques started back up the path, saying, "See you in a minute. I brought somethin' to show you."

I waited, but the cold began to crinkle the inside of my nose. As I moved toward the door Peter stepped out of the brush and stood looking toward the road. Jacques, a hundred-pound sack on one shoulder and a newspaper-wrapped parcel under the opposite arm, hove into view, followed by Ade, burdened with cedar like a faggot gatherer in a medieval engraving. Peter had smelled lunch from a distance.

Ade put branches under Peter's tree and Jacques carried the sack into our storage building. They had hardly closed the cabin door behind them when Peter settled his nose into the cedar.

"I brought him a sack of corn," Jacques said, watching Peter eat. "I didn't want to say anything 'til I knew he was still around. If he wasn't, he wouldn't be anywhere pretty soon, and I didn't want to make you feel any worse about it. This here"—he unwrapped the parcel—"is a leg off a little fawn I found frozen a week ago. Got into deep snow in a pocket and couldn't get out."

I looked at the sawed-off end of the frozen limb. Inside the creamy bone the marrow was red as blood.

"What caused that?"

"Starved. First the fat on their body goes, then the fat inside the bones. When they get like this . . ." He shook his head. "I was afraid your boy Peter was too far gone yesterday, but I knew you'd want to try to help him." He looked at Peter, yanking at the loose branches. "Don't seem to be able to figure out how to hold 'em with a hoof, does he? Ade, we'll fix him a real garden before I go."

Several cups of tea later Ade and Jacques drove away, to return with a truckload of cedar branches. They stacked most of them in the storage building and pushed the cut ends of a number of others firmly into the level snow above one of our garden plots; the green sprays looked like young trees growing there. Then they walked back and forth through the drifts to open a way between our hard-packed path and Peter's cedar garden.

"Anything that saves his energy, like that little trail, will help him," Jacques said as he turned to go. "And as long as it's this cold you can cut cedar ahead and it won't dry out."

Ade and I waved goodbye. Jacques was off to a lumber camp and we would not see him again until spring.

After lunch Ade had hardly settled to make some

sketches when he jumped up and stared, muttering, at the wall beside him. Water was trickling from the juncture of the topmost log and the slanting ceiling to reach the outermost curve of the largest log and drip from there to the floor. Heat from the stoves penetrates our not-too-well-insulated ceiling and melts the snow on the roof. When the water reaches the wide, unheated eaves some of it freezes on top of them and the rest forms a curtain of icicles. Usually Ade chips this ice away as soon as it forms, but this year he had been busier than usual and the ice had piled up faster. Its weight had opened the roofing seams.

While I mopped, with visions of reroofing next summer, Ade put his home-built ladder against the packed eave and chopped with hand ax and ice pick. My baking and his sketching waited and I thought of the man who had said to us, when he was helping us move our furniture into the cabins: "If you try to do anything on schedule up here, you'll go nuts!"

In the morning my first sight from the window was of Peter, nipping cedar in his garden. When he had enough he walked slowly and steadily, not shivering as he had the day before, along the paths toward the cabin. Then he bumped heavily against the base of the ladder, which Ade had left slanting from the edge of the snowshoe path to the roof, in position for more ice chipping. Peter stopped with one foot lifted, ears twitching and body trembling, not as one shakes from cold and hunger but more as one quivers from fright. The ladder was on his blind side and, although his good right eye gave him excellent vision to that side and to the front, he seemed not to know what had struck him, nor how to turn his head to find out.

I placed his corn, carrots, and suet under the big cedar tree and Peter timidly moved there to eat.

While Ade shifted the ladder away from the path, I thought over Peter's problem. His handicap would not lessen. Our feeding would not make him capable of independence if he did not learn how to cope with his one-sided blindness. He had managed to tell me that he wanted more food and that he liked carrots. Why should I not try to show him how to see to the left with an eye designed mainly for front and right-hand vision?

When he had finished eating and was standing quietly under his tree, I walked outside, repeating his name over and over. He twisted his ears toward the strange sound and, as I moved slowly in front of him and then turned to pass by his left side, he continued to follow the sound with his ears but did not turn his head. I stopped just behind his shoulder about five feet from him, still talking softly. Then I waved my arm slowly past the left side of his head, so that my hand moved beside and ahead of his nose. His right eye caught the movement and, as I drew my hand back to my side, he turned his head until, with his neck curved in a U-shape to the left, he was looking back at me with his right eye. After doing this for four days in succession, I omitted the hand waving and Peter followed the sound of my voice with both ears and eye. One day when I stood farther back than usual, almost even with his rump, he turned his head to the right and over his back to see me, his body and neck curving in the shape of a figure six.

From then on he investigated things on his left by twisting his head around, either to the left side or over his back, whichever was handiest. It is not unusual for deer to do this. Apparently Peter, either from the shock of his injury or from the confusion caused by his blindness, was afraid to look back or had forgotten how. It was not until years later, after I had watched other deer step away when I approached too near, that I was humbled by an understanding of Peter's amazing trust.

During his first two weeks with us, Peter changed greatly. His coat became smoother, his gauntness lessened, and he shivered only when the bitterest winds blew. His confidence in us did not lessen as he gained strength, and only once did we unintentionally frighten him.

Deer are said to be color-blind and we gave no thought as to the effect of what we wore. Then I had the bright idea of buying a bargain assortment of men's shirts from a mail-order house. Among them was a cream-colored affair, fuzzy, warm, and banded across the chest with inch-wide bars of green, black, yellow, and scarlet. Ade gave one look and said "Burn it!" I finally persuaded him to wear it out around the cabin in winter when we were unlikely to have visitors.

The first time he wore the thing he went out to feed Peter, who looked, snorted, and bounded into the brush. Color-blind or not, he reacted to patterns. The "deer-scarer" shirt is still in the bag where I keep scraps I some-day hope to make into a rag rug.

By the end of January Peter, although by no means heavy, was no thinner than many deer at the end of a hard winter. The small wounds on his head had disappeared, but there was a permanent notch on the outside edge of his right ear. He was still a little uncertain in his movements and would not lower his head to eat when red squirrels were near, perhaps because they had a way of jumping at his face and their sharp claws could easily damage his good eye. The alarm squalls of the blue jays, which are one of the most quickly heeded wilderness danger signals, always alerted him when he first came to us, but he soon distinguished between the jays' true alarms and their false alarms, which are a clear-the-deck technique to give them uncontested access to our feeding area. He had even adjusted to the sound of voices from the lake, where ice fishermen huddled against the wind, hopefully and sometimes successfully.

As long as the men were upwind and he could check their scent he showed no signs of nervousness, unless they began to walk toward our shore, which was also toward him. He made careful use of wind direction, turning toward the breeze when he fed under the trees, frequently lifting his head to test the air for messages. His garden lay south of the cabin, which both sheltered him from prevailing northerly winds and made locating the direction of a scent more difficult. When he fed there he frequently stepped past the corners of the cabin to listen and sniff. He had learned to ignore the many odors which lie around a human habitation.

One afternoon when Ade was out cutting cedar I heard the heavy thudding of hoofs approaching through the woods and opened the door to meet Peter's skidding arrival in front of the step. He snorted and tossed his head like a terrified horse and scattered the snow with heavy and repeated stomping of his front hoofs. I went out but could not see or hear anything unusual. Then I watched him lift his head, with nostrils widespread, toward the west. I, too, turned that way and smelled wood smoke.

Peter, still too weak for a run, stood panting. I followed our path westward under the big trees, past the summer house, down a slope, and across the wide sheet of ice that had formed when our little brook froze and overflowed in the fall. Just beyond, dangerously close to a small cabin which had once been an old woodsman's home, a fisherman, now settled out on the lake ice, had left an oversized campfire burning. As I scattered the blazing branch sections with a stick and covered them with snow, I wondered why Peter had come to "tell" me of the fire.

Deer are said to flee wood smoke instinctively, but they become accustomed to it, sometimes sheltering in the smoke of burning brush piles to escape the miseries of fly time. Peter was of course used to the smoke from our chimney. The sight of the flames may have frightened him, but I have no explanation for his rushing to spread the alarm. A fire in midwinter, when frost crystals have penetrated every crevice and cranny of the trees, is rarely dangerous to the forest. However, had this blaze been left on a breezy day when the snow was gone, Peter's warning could well have prevented a fire which would have burned us out, along with many square miles of forest.

As I ground an extra portion of carrots for him, I thought it a pity that research on game animals is so largely directed toward producing them, and that study of them as individuals is neglected. Men who were native to the forests in earlier days and who are now considered primitive had respect for their wild neighbors and learned from them. Much is lost by moderns who look on them only as things or meat.

As Peter learned to accept our queer odors, so also he became accustomed to human sounds, although more selectively. The loud clang when I accidentally dropped the heavy aluminum lid of my Dutch oven on the iron cookstove top only made him twitch his ears, but any thump, either inside the cabin or made by snow clumps dropping from high branches, brought him to a quick alert. Perhaps they resembled the deer's stomp, which I had first heard when Peter brought warning of the fire. When the wind was strong, he came near the cabin and listened nervously, apparently unable to separate sounds which might mean danger from the general wind noises. Only on nights like this did he sleep under his cedar tree as he had done on the first night he was with us. Perhaps he felt safer near the cabin and us. We like to think so.

The hubbub of a city passes over me as though it were not there because it is none of my business, but here sounds speak to people as well as to wild creatures. Noisy nights tend to make me restless because I, too, cannot distinguish one outside sound from another. My cure for compulsive listening to the wind is to turn on the battery radio. I had no idea that Peter, lying under his tree, would pay any attention to music until I went out one evening to put food in the woodshed for my flying squirrels and saw him sitting up with his ears turned to catch the strains of "Mood Indigo." He listened attentively until the program changed to a Strauss waltz. Then he lowered his head, laid his ears back, stood up, and stalked into the woods.

There is much talk of the January thaw, which is supposed to start evening up the first water for spring growth and which may actually arrive any time from December on. During Peter's first winter with us the thaw came on February third, a glorious, sunny, forty-five-degree day. While new icicles formed on the edge of the eaves Ade had so laboriously cleared a few weeks before and we stood outside, soaking up sun warmth, Bedelia set up a loud cackling.

"I'd better get her screen door or she'll yell all day," Ade said, and headed for the storage building.

Bedelia is a hen of character. She arrived along with twenty-three other month-old black chicks a year after we moved here and is still scratching around outside today at the ripe old age of ten years plus.

We originally planned to raise chickens for eggs and food but realized when the cold weather started that proper heating and housing for them in this climate would be almost impossible without, for us, too elaborate and uneconomical installations. We did try to set Bedelia once, but she looked at the nestful of eggs, gave an outraged squawk, and settled herself on the bare boards of the chickens' summer quarters. Eggs she would lay, but her responsibilities ended there.

So the chickens went the way of all flesh until only Bedelia was left. Her antics were so entertaining that we kept her as a pet and she rewarded us by supplying our essential eggs for the next six years.

Ade remodeled a small storage shed into a private cottage for her. He covered it inside and out with tar paper, fitted a small double-glass window in the door, and turned an old-fashioned oil lantern into a stove. This has a hood for fumes made from a wide stovepipe adapter, and a stovepipe chimney. He fitted a screen around the whole heating unit so that Bedelia could not catch her tail feathers on fire. He installed a perch and laying box, and lined the floor with dried grass. Then he built a little run, extending from the door and around one side of the house, and covered its sides and top with chick wire. It has a gate through which I can just manage to reach in to feed Bedelia, usually catching my hair on the wire in the process.

Once settled in her small domain, she became very self-sufficient and rapidly adjusted to woods life. Chipmunks and squirrels may rob her food tray, and bears peer at her with interest. Ermines may scoot around her feet while small birds perch on the wire above her head. She goes right on preening her color-washed black feathers. She will never like foxes, and it took her a long time to get used to the jays flying overhead, but now she has even lost most of her ancient fear of flying enemies and never sets up an alarm unless a big owl perches nearby.

On this particular day of early warmth, Bedelia's run was a foot deep in snow, so Ade opened her wooden door and fitted in her screen to let her get fresh air and enjoy the view, so to speak. All went well until Peter walked out of the woods.

He hesitated when he saw movement where there had not been movement before, then walked over and lowered his head to peer closely at this feathered creature. This was too much for Bedelia. Squawking and flapping, she managed to push out the screen, which Ade had not bothered to hook in place, and shot straight into Peter's face with

only the wire between them. He jerked back, caught his
rear hoofs in some way and sat down on his rump, jarring
the gate of the run open at the same time. Bedelia flew out
and up onto a branch, where she set up a wild clamor,
which was soon added to by the jays and squirrels. Ade
ran to get a length of wire, and bent one end of it into a
hook with which he could catch her by a leg, once he had
shaken her out of the tree onto the ground. Peter, staring
up at her as though incredulous, slowly rolled to one side,
folded his legs under himself, and got up. He walked, with
what dignity he had left, away from the coop and stood,
ignoring us all, until order was restored. And he never
again showed the slightest interest in Bedelia or her domain.

February 6
to Mid-February

·The thaw was short-lived and three nights later I stood alone in our clearing in windless, bitter cold. The light of a full moon turned the dusting of fallen frost into a glittering cover for the drifts. The black points of the evergreens reached toward the luminous faded-blue sky where a planet and three stars shone faintly golden. The treetops' deep purple shadows stretched like velvet bands across the snow, and darkness huddled under the trees—black, impenetrable, smothering. Anything might be waiting, watching there, but probably nothing was. On such a night the creatures of the forest take cover, both from the cold and the revealing light.

As I felt the chill penetrating my clothes, I hastily poured out grain from the can, which was almost frozen to my fingers. Peter and the flying squirrels would come out of the shadows when the moon was down. I slipped inside quietly because Ade was already asleep, and I thought for the thousandth time that the sleeplessness which had been a curse in urban daytime schedules was a blessing here, where it let me see the glories of the wilderness nights.

The moonlight streamed through the bedroom window and reflected from the mirror over the maple chest; it was so bright it showed the colors of my cross-stitched rugs and drew ghostly images from the varnished irregularities of the logs. This was a night for unfettered imaginings. With the lamp glowing on my night table, I settled down to read *Dracula*, in a forest which might well have been the prototype of the dark fictional one which surrounded the vampire's castle. I read on and on.

". . . I heard a sound in the courtyard without . . . the voice of the Count calling in his harsh metallic whisper. His call seemed to be answered from far and wide by the howling of wolves. . . ."

I dropped the book and jerked upright so sharply that my elbow almost overturned the lamp. I must be dreaming —I could *hear* those wolves! A chorus of their voices, moaning in different pitches, blending into a chorded song —coming near, getting louder. My throat was dry and my skin crawled. Then Ade sat up, yawned, and said, in a matter of fact way: "Wolves on the road, aren't there?" Dracula's werewolves vanished like popped bubbles as Ade turned over and went back to sleep.

Because we had been so interested in Peter and had heard no wolves so far during the winter, I had forgotten all about them. Now their voices were dying away toward the west as they trotted along the road. Still somewhat unnerved, I thought anxiously of Peter, not yet fully recovered, but I relaxed as I heard a breeze from the east stirring the trees. Peter would have scented the wolf family long before I could have heard them. He had no doubt removed himself from their path and might stay away for some time. I hoped he would find a way to come in safely for food, but that was deer business, not mine.

I blew out the lamp and looked into the dark forest. A few days before I had received a letter in which a friend wrote, *You seem to feel that nature is always smiling. Surely it has some sinister aspects.* A widespread but absurd idea. Nature simply is. Its smiles or frowns are reflections from the human mind.

In the morning the breeze had become a snow-laden wind. The tracks on the road were covered before we could learn how many wolves had passed by, and the wild creatures were competing for the grain buried in the clearing. The blue jays hissed at each other as they threshed through the snow with their beaks to uncover Peter's corn, until a squirrel scampered down a tree bole and scattered them. The squirrel nibbled steadily until a ruffed grouse dropped from a branch, puffed up its feathers, and bluffed the squirrel away. The grouse ate its breakfast, dodging occasional swoops by the blue jays, while the gray jays kept out of the squabble and begged for crackers at the door.

Peter walked into the yard at noon and took possession of the remains of his grain. He listened more than usual, sniffed the wind, jumped at sudden sounds. Then wolves howled across the lake in Canada. Peter twitched his ears, but with slight interest. Apparently he knew they were too distant to menace him. When others, presumably those I had heard in the night, lifted their melancholy voices not far away, he followed their location carefully, listening from one part of the yard, then another, going to the top of the hill by the road and reconnoitering, finally returning to finish his meal. When the wind veered to the north and he was upwind of the wolves, he bounded away.

Wolves may or may not seek out the weak, but they are most likely to catch animals least able to protect themselves for whatever reason—sickness, injury, old age, even immaturity and lack of experience. If Peter had not found us, if we had not fed him, no doubt the wolves would have had him weeks before; he was too feeble to have escaped them. Such an end might have been less miserable than starvation, but I could not be objective about this. The surge of relief I had felt when he returned safely to the yard told me how fond of him I had grown.

A few nights later I was wakened by the most dreadful sound I had ever heard, a hoarse scream that had a human quality. Icy with sweat, shaking, I sat up in bed and tried to locate it, but it moved through the woods, so muffled and distorted by the snow and air currents that it seemed to shift direction at each occurrence. At first I thought a man had become lost and was running in the kind of panic that can blot out all reason. Then, as the repetitions of the sound came nearer to the cabin, I caught a bleating undertone. It was a deer screaming, and the thing that sounded human was a note of mortal terror, which is the same in any creature's shriek of desperation.

I shook Ade awake. "Peter! Something's wrong with Peter!"

The terrible sound came again, now from the lake. We

reached the north window just as a wolf ran across the snow beneath, head out, tail flowing—death on silent feet. I whimpered and Ade caught my shaking hands.

"Get hold of yourself. It isn't Peter. Look—there on the ice."

A very small deer was struggling to keep its footing on the slippery surface. A wolf sprang on it from the rear. The deer slipped and fell. A second wolf closed in. There was one more scream, then silence and a huddled movement on the ice.

"There's something wrong," I babbled. "It doesn't look right—they might be ghosts—"

"You're scared silly," Ade said. "I'm thirsty. Make some tea."

He pushed me toward the kitchen, and ten minutes later, feeling the complete fool for my lapse into the superstitions of my ancestors, I handed Ade his cup and looked out the window again. The huddle was still there. And something still looked unnatural to me, although I refrained from saying so.

"Let's sit down," Ade said. "There isn't anything more to see."

"Or hear," I added, thankfully. "We'll go down in the morning and look around."

Hours later I was still awake, trying to figure out why I was so disturbed. It had been quick; no more than three minutes from the deer's first cry to the end. And such an end was far easier than that of a doe who had broken through rotten spring ice on the lake the year before and climbed up again and again, only to have the edge break away each time, until exhaustion let her slip under the water. Or another, who, rising on her hind feet to get cedar, had slipped and caught a foreleg between two small trees; her long struggle must have been agonizing before thirst ended it. There was nothing in this wolf kill to rouse such pity, or to shock me so deeply.

Then I realized that the savagery of the thing had temporarily stunned my reason. It was something so ruthless and violent that it is no longer within the comprehension of the normal human mind. But, savage as it had been, it was for the betterment of the group from which one deer was now gone. This was the natural way to prevent an overpopulation and starvation for many.

I was dropping off to sleep when I thought I heard a faint bleat, like that of a lamb. I jumped up and as I looked out into the pale light, Ade, who had not been able to sleep either, joined me. The tremulous sound came again.

"Behind Peter's tree," I whispered. "A fawn."

"The twin of the one that was killed—but where's the mother? It's too little and scared to take care of itself. It needs help."

As if in answer, a deer moved into our sight, not a doe, but Peter. He approached very slowly, making no sudden moves, as the fawn bleated, louder this time, and backed uncertainly away until its rump came up against our wood-pile and it stood as though it dared not turn aside. Peter came near, nosed its face gently, licked behind an ear, then stood quietly by its side. We scarcely breathed while the fawn lifted its head and timidly licked the side of his face. When he moved away, the fawn, now quiet and steady on its feet, followed.

We stepped outside and watched them walk deep into the forest.

Ade shook his head in amazement. "You could watch deer for a lifetime and they'd show you some new side of themselves every day. Do you suppose it's his fawn?"

I grinned. "Very doubtful. Bucks are of the Casanova type. He's just baby-sitting. Sometimes the things I see here give me a bewitched feeling."

"This is an enchanted night," Ade said. "Did you ever before see anything back inside the forest on a moonlit night?"

"No. Too many deep shadows. But it's light under the trees tonight!"

"And look at the ground. *We* aren't casting any shadows either."

The sky was so screened with swirling frost and the snow so thickly covered with its shining plates that the light of the moon was wholly and perfectly diffused. In the clearing and under the thickly branched trees, on our faces turned to the sky and on the snow behind us, there was a smooth, silvery, even glow.

"That's why I thought the wolf wasn't real," I said. "No shadow. Do you suppose nights like this started the superstition that werewolves and such cast no shadows?"

"Maybe. I don't feel very substantial without one myself."

The squalling of ravens woke me to a morning almost as shadowless as the night just past, with the dimness under the trees matching the cloud-covered sky and the chalk-white snow in the clearing reflecting soft light into the cabin. The big black birds were wrangling over shares of the frozen deer carcass. Ade and I went to the shore, and as we stepped onto the lake ice they flapped up noisily, to wheel overhead and croak a protest at the interruption of their feeding.

The wolves had eaten more than half of the fawn, but we could see that it was thin and undersized, too small to fight its way through the deep snow without great strain or to reach much of the tall browse.

"It probably would have starved before spring," Ade said. "Its twin looked stronger to me. Let's check the tracks and see how this happened. Then the ravens can get on with their job."

One wolf had driven the fawn from east to west, past the south side of the cabin, then had speeded up and deftly herded it northward toward the lake. The fawn had tried to turn back toward the east, but had been met by the wolf we had seen leaping past the north cabin window. Between them, the wolves had forced the fawn onto the ice, where its small hard hoofs could get no purchase and the wolves' big hairy paws gave them the advantage of sure-footedness. It had no chance in any case because it was neither large enough nor strong enough to run ahead of the wolves for more than a short distance.

Near midnight, when Peter's untouched grain told me that he was still discreetly absent, I saw the wolves finishing their prey. In the morning the snow that the heavy clouds had promised the day before was starting to fall, fine and vertical, but with the murmur of a distant wind. The ravens' harsh voices were missing. I hurried to the shore to see what remained of the drama before the drifting crystals should obliterate it.

The fawn was gone. Scattered on the trodden and moiled snow surface were tufts of hair, splinters of bone, and bright scarlet patches of frozen blood. The tracks of the two wolves led away across the lake, walking, then trotting, headed for the far shore. The larger forepaw tracks, presumably those of a male, were six inches long, and his slow trotting stride was thirty-four inches. No wonder this big and powerful animal had stirred atavistic fears in me when he had passed, shadowless, just beneath the window where I watched. The forepaw tracks of the other, probably his mate, were four and a half inches long, and her stride was twenty-three inches. From the size of the tracks and their depth in the snow layer on the ice I estimated their weights to be, respectively, about one hundred thirty and ninety pounds. They were giants among Minnesota timber wolves, whose average weight, the sexes not separated, is roughly eighty pounds.

As the snow began to blur the tracks and turn the view to the north into white nothingness, a howl drifted to me on the rising wind, to be joined almost at once by another, lighter voice. The same wolves? Perhaps. I imagined them, deep inside the shifting snowfall, heads up, ears cocked, bushy tails flowing behind them as their long legs made light of the hilly miles, hunting, always hunting in their phase of the struggle for existence.

Mid-February
to April 7

In the morning the cabin was full of a delicious scent blended from birch smoke and fresh coffee, and I had a strong feeling that some pleasant change had taken place. This did not make much sense until I noticed the long, pale beam of sunlight, slanting through the living room's east window. Not since early November had the sun's rising point been far enough north and its arc high enough to send morning light through that window. Responding to this advance notice of spring, I carried a cup of coffee outside to watch Ade feeding the birds.

He coaxed the gray jays down to his fingers for crackers, while the blue jays perched in the trees and conversed in their spring voices—clicks and buzzes and little flutelike notes. Two male downy woodpeckers argued in spirited squeals for first place at a hanging suet feeder, their head patches glowing ruby-bright as they moved in and out of a ray of sunlight. A red squirrel dropped from a branch onto the woodshed roof, plopped to the feeding shelf beside the door, and waved a paw toward me. I took a cracker from Ade and poked it into the mouth of the squirrel, who grasped it between his thumbless hands, squeaked politely, and settled back to nibble.

I saw the wide-spaced, neatly pared tracks of a bounding ermine and watched a snowshoe hare scamper across the hill like a boisterous snowball. In the distance a pileated woodpecker whacked away at some rotten bole or stump, hunting carpenter ants for breakfast. I thought of people who have said to me: "From Christmas until April in the woods is just a long drag." How much they miss, sitting inside with a radio constantly murmuring for company, never feeling the thrill of the first sun over the treetops, hardly aware of the busy forest life all around.

"Three spruce grouse were here earlier," Ade said. "They took off when I came out. I saw the red on the male's head."

"We had a special visitor before that," I said, beckoning him to follow me around the cabin. "There." I pointed to a line of tiny deer tracks spaced between larger ones.

"The big ones look small for Peter," he said, bending to look more closely at the heart-shaped marks.

"Naturally. They aren't Peter's. The doe came at first light for her youngster. I had a good view of him—a little buck with hair swirls where his antlers will grow. The lower half of his front legs is white. They're almost invisible against the snow. I've named him Snowboots. I saw Peter, too, under his tree. I think he brought the little guy back and the doe may have been waiting."

We walked to Peter's tree, where there were other deer tracks, large and clear. On the outside of the right front hoof was a double notch, which must have been caused by some accident during the first three or four days of Peter's life, when his hoofs had not yet fully hardened from their soft pre-birth condition. We had not seen his tracks before in snow that took a clean impression, but now we could recognize them wherever and whenever we should come upon them. His notched hoof was as distinguishing an identification mark as a fingerprint.

As the days brightened and lengthened toward the end of February the pattern of forest life began to change. The gray jays, unmindful of cold and snow, disappeared into the dense spruce tops to nest, reappearing now and then to pull strips of cedar underbark for building material and to snatch hasty meals in the yard. The barred owls, who enlivened the winter nights with their deep "Who-*who*-waaaah! You-*you*-aaaall!" set up a lively cackling and grunting, with periods of weird and noisy hooting. This, in late winter, is their voice of tenderness. One pair did their courting on a branch of the big pine west of the cabin, bobbing and bowing to each other while flapping their wings and filling the air with full-voiced hoots that surely could be heard for miles through the otherwise-silent night. Soon the owls went away to take over their old nests, very casually made in tree hollows or abandoned hawks' nests and often used until they are so dilapidated that they can no longer safely hold either eggs or young birds. Regardless of their housekeeping, our owls do well enough with their broods to keep the forest adequately supplied with interesting and invaluable rodent controllers.

Peter stayed near the clearing, eating his large measure of cedar, his small measure of corn, his assorted vegetable scraps and suet, and his carrots, which always set him shaking his ears and prancing like a fawn—behavior both incongruous and delightful in a dignified buck, now fattened up to around two hundred pounds. By the middle of March he showed no sign of his ordeal by starvation. His coat was smooth, his body blocky and strong, his face beautiful. He held his blind eye so nearly open that it was noticeable only by its lack of light, and he began to roam the forest, usually coming to the yard once each day for a good meal.

One evening as he was nipping his cedar, another deer, slim, long-legged, with a winter coat more brown than gray, stepped from the forest to the bank which formed its edge and was also the side of a ditch, dug to divert water from the lower land of the log cabin's yard. The newcomer scratched behind his ear with a hind leg and we saw from his underparts that he was a buck. This was sheer luck because it is not easy to tell a whitetail doe from a buck whose antlers have dropped and not yet started new growth. Bucks may be larger and have relatively narrower rumps, but not always. There is a slight difference in the positions of tail and hip bones, but this is hidden by the hairs of the coat. The skeletal structure of the head is somewhat different, the buck's nose bridge usually being higher and straighter, but the profiles are not reliably different. The fur on the buck's head may grow in a flatter shape, showing somewhat fuzzy low rises on the forehead where the bony rings called pedicels wait to put forth new antlers, and, for a time after the antlers have fallen, the pedicels may be seen in the fur. However, an adult deer with a narrow, somewhat short face and a head smoothly rounded between the ears is likely to be a doe.

Peter glanced up at the buck on the bank and returned to his feeding. The newcomer leaped down into the garden, pivoted on his hind legs, and struck down at the snow in front of Peter, who snorted, lifted a foreleg to stomp solidly, and walked over until he was almost touching noses with the newcomer. I wondered if they would fight, this not being the rutting season with its attendant touchy temper in bucks. They stood unmoving for several minutes, whereupon Peter stepped back and began to eat and the other bent his head to take his share of the cedar. Apparently they had settled matters to their mutual satisfaction because when the cedar was almost gone Peter moved away into the woods with his new friend at his heels.

Just after sundown, I was surprised and pleased to see young Snowboots, thinner than he should be, walk cautiously into the cedar garden, which Ade had replenished with fresh branches. Peter and Friend appeared at the edge of the brush across the clearing at the same time. Friend bounded into the garden almost on top of Snowboots, who fled without getting a bite, Friend hard after him. Peter ran diagonally through the woods in magnificent leaps, cut in front of Friend, and blocked him long enough for Snowboots to get away. Then Peter returned to feed quietly on the cedar and Friend followed shortly after, but not to feed quietly. He stomped and snorted, pulled up the branches, and generally expressed displeasure at the whole proceeding. Peter finally whirled and struck in his direction—a sort of last warning, maybe—and walked over to chew his cud under his tree. Friend subsided, and I thought that their personalities varied even more than their appearance.

The next afternoon, while Ade was out cutting cedar and the bucks were gone, I saw Snowboots deep in the woods with his mother close by. She had a distinctive stance, head lifted and thrust forward, ears so twisted to listen for sounds from both cabin and road that she looked vaguely as though she wore one of those gallantly tip-tilted hats peculiar to Australia. And she stomped—and stomped and stomped. At last convinced that there was no imminent danger, she reared on her hind legs to reach and break down a high cedar branch. Snowboots leaped forward and buried his nose in the fresh and fragrant green. Only when he had eaten most of it did his mother step forward to clean up the leaf fragments that remained on the twigs.

Deer do not rear up for browse unless they need it badly. Instinct seems to warn them that there is danger of injury from falls, even of impalement on sharp branches. As the doe reached up again, I considered how best to help these two, who I thought had had their share of trouble. Grain and cedar could always be found near the cabin, but there had been no tracks of doe and fawn since she had come for Snowboots after his twin was killed. If hunger had not driven her to bring her youngster to our feeding place so far, it probably would not in the future. And Friend would drive them away if he could.

When Ade came back with his cedar, I put the problem up to him.

"Simple," he said. "It won't be much more work to get more cedar. I'll make another garden. Where were they?" I pointed out the place. "Fine. It isn't so shaded that we can't see who eats the stuff."

The new little patch of upright branches looked very

enticing in the open spot surrounded by big trees. I did not leave the window until the evening shadows turned from translucent blue to opaque gray.

We had just finished our dinner when Ade said: "What's that?"

I listened. Thump—thump—thump, spaced and firm on the frozen ground.

"The doe—stomping. Blow out the lamp. There's a young moon."

She moved in the soft light, a pale and wary wraith, stomping, listening, sniffing the air, the snow, the cedar. At length she turned toward the trees and Snowboots leaped from their shelter, his "invisible" front legs identifying him as clearly as the twisting ears and uplifted head identified his mother. There was enough food for both. They were standing quietly, chewing their cuds together, probably free of hunger for the first time in many days, when a cloud bank rolled up from the south like the smoke of a vast campfire and hid them under its shadow.

The wind that brought the clouds was warm and the morning temperature was well above freezing. Chickadees gave their vernal call that sounds like "Spring's here—spring's here." Loosened snow dropped from the trees and floated, glittering, to tickle my face as I looked up to see the long rays of the sun strike fire from the pine tops. A breeze brought the scent of rosin to us for the first time since the beginning of winter. A pair of red squirrels started an early courtship and chased each other in a spiral round and round a balsam trunk. The great cycle of forest life was approaching its full swing again.

Peter and Friend began to roam farther and sometimes did not come to the yard for several days. Then they fed quietly together in the cedar garden, after which Friend went back into the woods while Peter came to the cabin for his grain and carrots. Friend would tolerate us from a distance, but he would never trust us as Peter did.

Occasionally Snowboots, whose legs were lengthening at an amazing speed, approached the bank when Ade and I were outside as though he wanted to see what we were doing. This was always nipped in the bud by his mother, who chased after him, whacked him soundly on the rump with a hoof, and herded him back into the forest. Plainly, a wise doe kept her child out of people's way.

Now Ade and I were bursting with plans—for transplanting wild flowers, painting the screens, taking off the heavy plastic sheets that give us a dead-air insulating space and are easier to handle than storm windows. I even dreamed of opening the windows and letting the fresh breezes clear away the staleness that lingered in the tightly closed cabin. But one day was freezing and damp, the next warm and drizzly, the next white with soggy snow. The shining days were few, but they dwarfed the others in our thoughts.

Humans began to stir. Cars moved on the road, somewhat mysteriously because the lodges beyond us were still untenanted. The road-maintenance crew used a steam hose to clear the ice from the culvert that carried our little brook under the road. Then Jacques came whistling down the path. The thaw had softened the snow in the deep woods and stopped the winter lumbering.

While we were sitting over tea and cookies, exchanging the bits of news that fill in the gaps left by the local newspaper, Jacques looked out of the window and almost dropped his cup.

"There's a big buck out there!"

"That," Ade said smugly, "is the one-eyed jack."

While Ade gave a summary of Peter's winter and Jacques gawked, I went into the kitchen to grind carrots and measure grain from the cans under the counter.

". . . and the oil truck brought us up a couple of sacks of corn and scratch feed," Ade finished.

"Now watch," I said, and opened the door.

Peter's ears twitched, the tip of his tongue showed pink against his black muzzle, and he walked sedately to the door and peered inside as I picked up the box lid that held his grain. He backed up a step to let me go out and pour the grain on the snow. Then he bent down to eat, so near that I could have buried my fingers in his thick, slate-gray coat. When the grain was finished he looked up expectantly and I brought him his carrots. Those eaten, and his appreciation adequately expressed by a toss of his head and a little bouncy step, he walked over to stand under his tree and chew his cud.

Jacques was shaking his head when I rejoined the men.

"I was born in the woods, but I never thought I'd see that. I've seen tame deer raised from fawns, but I never thought a grown buck would take to people. He comes up to you like a horse! How'd you get him trained?"

"I didn't train him," I said. "I let him train me. He's a wild animal like all the others. I give them food, and fit my actions to theirs. It's the only way to learn to know them."

Day by day the snow level dropped in spite of fresh falls. A little flock of juncos, the vanguard of the migrating birds, stopped to feed and rest in the yard, then flew on northward a week later. There was rain, and slush began to gray the surface of the now rotting lake ice. The acrid anise-tinged scent of wet wood and bark was in the air and, at night when the creatures of the forest were silent, we heard the gurgling of the brook, as its rising waters hunted passage through the already honeycombed earth. Ade came back from his trek for mail with the news that lodges were being readied for the tourist season to come.

Then the cedar that Ade put out for Snowboots and his mother remained untouched. With the coming of increased human activity, they had quietly vanished into the forest. Peter fed hastily, keeping his eye on Friend, who no longer came from the hill to the cedar garden. If Friend walked away, Peter trotted after him. The time was near for bucks to leave for the secret places where they spend the summer, and Peter did not seem to want to go alone. I wondered if he still felt somewhat insecure because of his one eye, if he might need Friend to aid him, once he was away from the wintering place that was so familiar. Perhaps he just wanted companionship. I shall never know, because I am not a deer.

On the cloudy morning of April seventh, when Ade was polishing windowpanes and I was making an assault on my shelves and shelves of dusty books, we heard Peter tapping on the step. This was his first morning visit since his early starvation days. I went out with grain, but he only licked off the top of it, then stood looking around and sniffing the air. Up on the hill, half-hidden by the budding maple, Friend was slowly moving toward the east. Ade joined me outside as Peter walked away on the path. He stopped at a place where an animal trail crosses our human trail, and stood motionless, looking back at us. Then he followed his companion into the forest.

the
second
year

MAMA AND HER TWINS

December 1
to December 24

I pulled the last page of a children's story from my typewriter. The yellow sheets on the light green of the kitchen table made a springtime color combination well suited to the robins in the story but pretty alien to our snowy December-first night. As I checked the word count, I considered my efforts at trying to find an ideal writing location.

First, the summer-house screened porch—airy, secluded; but so restful that I dreamily watched the trees, the birds, the gentle movement of the lake against the shore, and wrote not at all. Next, the west window of the summer house—brilliantly lighted, quiet; but so warmed by the afternoon sun that I grew sleepy. Then a south window of the log cabin—well lighted, out of the line of travel in this very small house; but perfectly located to catch sounds from the road. And no one ignores these in an isolated place, where the infrequent passerby may need help or directions.

The kitchen-table location had no disadvantage except that the drafty outside door on my right had a tendency to stick or pop open by itself under the influence of frost pressure on the foundation beneath it, and so could not be weather-stripped.

On this particular night, Ade had hit upon the excellent idea of preventing the forcible entry of the outside cold by stuffing the side of the door with folded newspapers and dragging a rug up against the bottom crack. Consequently, I was enjoying warm feet while he sat at the living-room table and applied first aid to our battery radio, which had developed the disconcerting habit of alternately blaring and whispering.

I pushed the typewriter aside, clipped my typed pages together, and stood up to stretch. I looked at the lamp—cast-iron base, patterned glass oil bowl, hand-blown chimney delicate as a bubble—and wondered how it had survived its eighty, perhaps ninety years. As I bent to blow it out there was a sharp rap on the door.

It didn't sound like a knock. It came again, near the top of the door. It was late, too late for ordinary visitors, and a deep awareness of the mystery of the wilderness outside sent a prickling across the back of my neck. Mindful that fear of the unknown must have no place in lives like Ade's and mine, I pulled back the curtain and looked through the glass panel—straight into Peter's face. He did not stir as I removed the makeshift draft stoppers and opened the door.

I drew a deep breath and stepped aside to let the lamplight flow over his strong, heavy body, his neck so thickened for the rutting that his face looked disproportionately small. And his antlers—almost as wide as the door, with

thirteen points, some lifting more than a foot above the main beams. Five tines on one beam, six on the other, a tall spike rising from each near the place where the antlers grew from his head. The thin and starving Peter we had once known was hard to find in this forest king in full mating armament, but I knew his gentle face, his blind left eye, his notched right ear.

His ears flipped in the direction of the living room and I heard Ade walking toward the kitchen.

"Fresh air is fine but—good Lord!"

Peter ducked his head, the great antlers which had earlier knocked against the door now reaching past the lintel into the room. He tapped on the step with a hoof and showed the tip of his tongue. In his own way he was telling us that he had come for supper.

He ate by the step and chewed his cud under his tree as he had done before. Then he explored the yard carefully, examining every little change—the big GI can which held a convenient supply of grain near Bedelia's house, a new hanging bird feeder, the open space left between two small trees when Ade stacked the firewood elsewhere. After the cabin was dark, I heard the tap of his antlers against the logs as he completed his survey by walking around the foundation and nosing into the woodshed.

We could not even guess at Peter's age the previous year because of his desperate physical condition. Bucks mature at two years but do not reach full size until three years later. Does mature and reach full size at two years. The average full weight for the large whitetail species found in Minnesota is approximately two hundred pounds for bucks, one hundred thirty pounds for does.

Now the development of Peter's neck and antlers showed him to be in the fullness of his maturity. The thickness of his antler beams at the base and the many small points and knobs that grew on that part of the beams indicated that he was not young. He was perhaps eight or nine years old.

The annual renewal of a buck's antlers will never cease to astonish me, but not until the summer when I was writing this did I have a chance to watch part of the process.

When most of the deer left in the spring, two yearling bucks stayed around and occasionally came for grain. One of these, named Whiskers, for a thick fringe of fur that ringed his jaws, had fed here through the winter. The other came out of the woods in March, rather poorly nourished, and became Whiskers' companion. When a female mallard discovered the grain in May, the last-arrived young buck seemed determined to learn just what this feathered thing was. Every time the duck appeared he hurried after her, closing in until she became alarmed and flew, leaving the frustrated Duck Hunter fidgeting as though he resented his lack of wings.

Near the first of April, dark gray bumps appeared on both Whiskers' and Duck Hunter's heads, slightly in front of and between the ears, pushing the reddish hair of the tufts aside as they rose from the pedicels. This growth is stimulated by the effect of increasing light on ductless glands and the development is so rapid that the antlers may reach full size in less than five months. The result, however, may vary greatly.

By the middle of May, Whiskers' antlers were three-inch single spikes, but those of Duck Hunter were only one third as tall. The growing antlers were covered by the layer of thick, fuzzy skin called velvet, which carries their blood supply. During the whole growing time the antlers would be soft and easily deformed or injured. Does need only threaten to butt or strike at such tender growths to chase away bucks during fawning time and the months when the nursing fawn is getting its first lessons in woods life.

In June, Whiskers' antlers spread at the top into a velvet-covered fan, which soon separated as the main beam curved upward and forward in its exquisitely graceful shape. A month later, the antler tips fanned and separated again, to form the second tine on each. Meanwhile, Duck Hunter had slowly produced upright main beams, about six inches tall, each with a small tine at the tip.

The yearlings departed before the end of August, when the antlers harden and the bucks rub the velvet off against trees and brush. This may take one or several days, during which the antlers look as though they are draped with old-man's-beard or shreds of bark. When the last velvet is gone and the antlers are polished, the buck is the handsomest fellow in the woods.

The antlers may be the two single points of the spike buck, or may have the Y-formation of Duck Hunter's. The number of points does not indicate a buck's age and sometimes first antlers, fully developed at one and a half years, have six or more points, as did Whiskers', and those of Pig and Brother, whom you will meet in the next chapter. Again, antlers may increase in the buck's first years from two points to a maximum number, which varies with the individual, at about five years. Often one beam has one more tine than the other, usually short and near the tip. Injuries or disease may cause irregular or malformed antlers. Racks are affected by both heredity and nourishment and perhaps our feeding helped Peter grow his magnificent set of weapons.

It may seem that I took dangerous chances when I stood beside Peter while he ate and sometimes held cedar branches down from the trees for his convenience when those of his garden were temporarily depleted. Bucks in rut are unpredictable and are said to be so as long as they carry their antlers. Peter's antlers could have gored as fatally as a bull's horns and a slashing blow from a sharp front hoof could have caused a mortal wound. But I think he had finished his season of fighting for the favor of the does when he came back to us this first time. He did not wander far and I often saw him slowly walking through the brush on the hill, pulling down twigs from the maples. Once he stood near the shore looking toward Canada. Perhaps he was considering the potentialities of emigrating. When he walked along our path, his head moving forward and back with each deliberate step and held high as though to balance his great rack, I was conscious only of his beauty and strength and dignity. Call me illogical if you will. To me he was my friend Peter, and I could never bring myself to fear him.

On the eighth of December, when he was eating in the yard, a chattering squirrel climbed one of his legs. He stomped and jolted off this trespasser, as a black-capped chickadee settled on one of his antler beams, protesting his consumption of corn in a strident bass. Peter, looking slightly astonished, raised his head. The chickadee, in front of his ear, appeared to be yelling into an old-fashioned ear trumpet. This was too much for Peter's sensitive hearing. He jerked his head and the antler dropped, with the little bird hanging on and complaining loudly. Peter, his head cocked a little to one side to balance the remaining antler, strolled into the woods.

The fallen antler was very hard and smooth-surfaced, with many ridges which began near the base of the tines and deepened toward the lower end of the main beam, where the spikes and knobs protruded. Although it had looked very light in color when sunlight contrasted it with Peter's dark head, only the highly polished tips of the tines were creamy white. Overall, it was a soft grayish-brown, with darker brown streakings in the hollows between the ridges.

At the base was a central, rounded protrusion of white, very porous bone, slightly dotted with blood. This continuation of Peter's skull had broken away from within the pedicel, when the bone underneath was resorbed. Around this spongy center was a flared and rippled flange of hard bone, which had separated from the pedicel's ring. This continued upward to form the outer covering of the antler and was, near the base, between a quarter and a half inch thick.

I noticed a heavy, musky fragrance which came not only from the porous center of the antler but also from its whole outer surface. This scent is very tenacious. As I write, I have an antler on my desk, dropped eleven months ago by Starface, Peter's son, of whom more later. Its scent is still so strong that it transfers to my fingers at the slightest handling.

I brought Peter's antler inside to Ade, who would surely want to weigh, measure, and sketch it.

"Now?" he asked, looking up from the board he was planing.

Surrounding him in a section of the cabin that adjoins the kitchen were piles of rough lumber, matched and numbered finished boards, and scatterings of sawdust and shavings. He was in the midst of building a set of bookshelves that eventually would be a room separator, high as the walls and open on both sides so that it would hold twice as many books, back to back. Books gravitate to me from friends, stores, and the exchanges that help out the winter reading situation here. Considering that the three hundred I had moved from Chicago were now lost among more than three thousand, many of which were piled on the floor, the bookcases seemed more important than sketching an antler, especially since we badly needed the space being used as a carpenter's shop.

"Oh no," I said hastily. "Anytime."

As he sighed and slid the plane along the board again, I looked around and saw no place to put the antler. So, not knowing as much about the woods as I do now, I put it outside under the storage building. When Ade went to get it in the spring, he found only fragments and a gnawed portion of the main beam. The crowd of rodents attracted by our yardful of grain—mice, voles, hares, squirrels, and, when they came out of their winter retirement, chipmunks —had demolished it for its calcium and phosphorus. With so many of these gnawing creatures in wild places, it is not surprising that one rarely finds antlers.

Peter came to the yard without his other antler four

days later. A little blood had trickled from the pedicel and frozen, to lie between his eyes like a ruby pendant. The raw place was scabbed over the next day and healed a week after.

Peter's antlers fell early, bucks losing their weapons from December until, in scattered instances, as late as March. Large antlers often drop earlier than small ones, but this is by no means the rule. There is some evidence that more frequent mating is related to early dropping of the antlers. Again, perhaps nutrition is a deciding factor, or antler weight. There is much to be learned about this and other phases of the lives of whitetails.

A week after Peter lost his second antler, I went out into the night to give some oatmeal to a flying squirrel who had glided to a noisy landing against the kitchen door. The beam of my flashlight struck into a world of fantasy. Snow was falling slowly, each flake so delicate and light that it drifted and turned in the air. The ground was covered by points of white fire with minute flares of red and green, purple and blue and gold, ever changing, as when drops of water, lingering on leaves after a shower, separate rainbow colors from sunlight. The tree trunks sparkled like crystalline pillars. Deep in the forest, where gray shadows thickened with distance and my light barely penetrated, scattered fairy stars twinkled. The very air glittered. A barred owl rose soundlessly from the woodpile, its wings spanning four feet of air, to cross the clearing like a coruscating phoenix, outlined by diamond-bright sparks.

I dropped to my knees to look closely at a thin scatter-

ing of the flakes that clung to the steep-slanted black blade
of the snow shovel, standing by the cabin door. Every
flake was a six-pointed star, intricately branched and orna-
mented. Some were so small that I longed for a magnifier;
some were a half inch across; all were perfect. As I looked
from one to the other of this small sampling of beauty
from the myriads that were scattered prodigally across the
land, a wind began to whistle from the northeast. The delicate stars swirled in the air and shattered as they were
blown along the ground. The red alcohol of the thermometer dropped as I watched. The snow began to come like
white cornmeal. I thought of a Cree Indian saying: "Snow
like meal, snow a great deal," and went to bed. `

The morning light looked into the cabin past triangles
of snow arranged artistically at the intersections of the
wooden strips that separate the small panes of our windows. The wind, working through the night with the foot
of newfallen snow, had covered the clearing with sculp-
ture. A long white wave, its top curled over, was caught
at the moment of breaking. A range of three-foot moun-
tains, their jagged peaks streaked with shadows the color
of glacier ice, crossed our path. A stump was girdled by a
straight and even white wall with a small opening like an
arched doorway in its leeward side. The snow had lifted
and hurried away along the ground in the hollows between
the drifts so that some places were nearly bare and showed
the green of sweet Williams, frozen solid and destined to
regrow from the roots, now that their blanket was removed. Squirrel tracks appeared mysteriously in the middle
of trackless spaces, continued for a short way and then

stopped abruptly, as their makers crossed patches of snow packed so solidly that their slight weight made no impression on the surface.

Under the trees eighteen squirrels were chattering, squealing, fighting. Sharp claws flashed and drops of blood spattered as those who customarily fed here reared onto their hind legs and fought to hold their territory against the invaders from the forest. Ade swept snow and squirrels together from our paths. I followed, dropping cracked corn, oatmeal, and graham crackers in little heaps along the cleared space, until the blue and gray jays sailed into the cedars, dislodging snow which poured down my neck and sent me in to change my shirt. By the time Ade had refilled the suet cages, our regular group of hairy and downy woodpeckers, brown- and black-capped chickadees, rose-breasted nuthatches, and ruffed grouse were busily eating. Then Peter walked casually through the assemblage, looking as large as Gulliver in Lilliput.

He was waiting at the step when he suddenly tightened his muscles as though to leap away, pulled back his head, spread his ears wide, and stared at the woodshed's foundation. A weasel, ermine-white and stretching up to all of eight inches, was returning the stare from interested black eyes. Peter gave a little snort and the weasel, with a flip of its black tail tip, popped into a snow tunnel, poked its head out at various points in the yard as though to annoy the squirrels, and vanished into a mouse hole under some roots. Peter was eating his cedar when the weasel emerged, a fat mouse in its jaws. It hopped to the ridge of a big drift and sat up, as though proud of its catch and wanting it to be properly admired. Then, neck arched like that of a carrousel horse, head high to keep the dangling mouse out of the way of its pattering front feet, it bounded toward its home in a leisurely manner.

As Peter was walking away from his garden he suddenly blew, reared, and slammed his front feet down. A brown streak shot away—somebody's Siamese cat, from where I have no idea, whose career had almost been cut short. With ears laid back, Peter blew again and trotted out of sight.

This blowing sound, made by forcing air through the nostrils violently and with considerable noise, is strictly an alarm or threat. I have heard it many times and, on those occasions when I was able to locate the cause, found that it could mean the near presence of lynx, bobcat, black bear, strange human, or domestic cat or dog. Sometimes foxes are blown at, but not always. I have never heard it when wolves were in the area, possibly because the deer scent the wolves and withdraw before these carnivores are near enough to create a need to spread an alarm by sound. An individual cut off from a herd and running from wolves would be unlikely to waste breath in blowing.

In the afternoon a man from Minneapolis who had managed to drive through the drifts, only to take a wrong turn, saw Ade's tracks leading from the road and came to ask directions. He was much excited by wide-spaced, deep tracks on our path, such as he had been told were made by wolves. Alarmed at the thought of danger to Peter, we hurried to see the tracks. Ade smiled, carefully removed the top snow from around one of them, and showed our visitor the pair of pointed marks made by the tip of one of Peter's hoofs.

After the man had gone on his way, having first been warmed with coffee and supplied with a map, I went out to look at Peter's tracks. One usually thinks of deer tracks as heart-shaped with a separation between the two halves, rounded at the back and pointed at the front. Some of Peter's tracks, in places where the snow had barely whitened the ground, were like that. On surfaces slippery with packed snow, the two parts of the hoof, which correspond to our third and fourth fingers, were splayed wide apart and the soft, hairy underpart of the hoof acted as a nonskid device. On slopes where this had not been enough to prevent skidding, he had flattened his hoof so that the dew claws, small black-tipped toes corresponding to our index and little fingers and located some four inches above ground on the back of each foot, dug into the snow and acted as brakes. (The digit which would correspond to the human thumb has disappeared.) On a smooth, flat surface covered by about an inch of snow I saw the long, twin drag marks behind each hoof print which are sometimes made by the walking buck. Does and fawns tend to lift their feet higher and rarely so mark thin snow layers. In deep snow, drag becomes a downward diagonal slash, made by all deer as their hoofs plunge forward as they walk.

The road was plowed and smooth when Ade walked up to get our mail on the morning of Christmas Eve. I was remembering Peter as he had been the previous Christmas when I looked out of a window and saw a strange man standing on our path with his back to me. He wore the boots, stag pants, and plaid jacket of a woodsman, and as he turned from looking into the brush I did a double take. He carried a rifle across his arms. I went out.

"Looking for someone?" I asked, walking toward him.

He jumped and whirled to face me. "I saw the tracks going out. Didn't know anybody was here—wouldn't want to bother you," he mumbled.

"Oh? What do you want?"

"I—uh—heard you had a tame buck. Thought I'd like to take a look at him."

We were ten feet apart and I was staring at the rifle— a .30–.30 with the safety off. My heart began to thump and I felt strangely light-headed.

"With that thing? Get out!"

There was a silence. Then he pointed the rifle at me and, with some exceptionally colorful obscenities, ordered me into the house.

I obeyed, slid a clip into a heavy automatic pistol, and stepped outside, the gun behind my back. I turned cold as I saw Peter, stiffly alert and with ears turned forward, standing by the storage building, just out of the poacher's sight. With an effort I managed not to turn my head in that direction and walked slowly toward the intruder.

"Still here?" I asked in what I think was an ordinary tone.

The man smirked in that exaggerated, nasty way I had thought was peculiar only to TV villains and started to raise the rifle again. I snapped the pistol around in front of me and thumbed back the hammer.

The smirk melted. "I was only kiddin', lady. Be careful! You might hurt somebody!" And he took off up the path with me at his heels.

Ordinarily it would have been quite impossible for me to run up that steep slope in deep snow, but this time I seemed to fly. I reached the top as a pick-up truck with no rear license plate rattled away.

I was halfway back to the house when my knees started to shake and I sat down in the snow. Shades of Calamity Jane! What a ridiculous and melodramatic scene for me to be playing. As the light-headedness went away, I recognized it as a symptom of a cold fury I would not have thought myself capable of. I looked up and saw Peter walking toward me. Mentally thanking my father for having taught me to handle guns when I was hardly big enough to lift one, I eased the pistol hammer down and stood up.

"Peter," I said seriously, "I have just pulled off the year's most important bluff." He turned his ears in my direction and cocked his head. "Nobody will ever eat you for dinner if I can help it. That's a promise."

January

The oil stove mumbled softly inside the cabin. Outside, sporadic sharp reports, like distant shots, ripped the silence of the January night as tree trunks burst under the pressure of the frost. The roof snapped as though the ridgepole were breaking. Ade turned over in his sleep and I thought of our alarm when we had first heard such cabin sounds, and of how we had searched to find the damage. We never found any. The noises were those of logs contracting and expanding, of roofing moved by some shift of the building. At any rate, this night was getting very cold.

I threw on a jacket and went out to make sure that Bedelia's lantern-heater was functioning properly. Lantern flames have a way of changing height with temperature and moisture variations, and I had no wish to find our pet hen either frozen or suffocated in the morning. Bedelia gave me what seemed like a sleepy and annoyed glance from her perch, as though she did not appreciate my solicitude. I turned away from her little house to see Peter walking down the path. He would no doubt like some extra corn on such a cold night. I went inside for it and stopped to warm my tingling fingers over the oil stove.

As I started to step back out I caught the white flashes of two tails as their owners dived into the brush, and saw a doe turning on her hind legs to follow. Peter leaped halfway across the yard and landed directly in front of her, knees bent and body tense. She jerked back. He straightened up and faced her, his ears turned forward. She hesitated, looking uneasily at me in the doorway, then turned to him, her ears in the same forward position. I counted thirty-five seconds during which they did not move. Then, as though communication had been completed, both relaxed and their ears went back to the ordinary position.

Icy air was rapidly filling the cabin and I decided that I had best take out the feed. While I moved slowly to and from Peter's tree, he waited quietly fifteen feet from the tree and the doe stood her ground beside him, although she twitched occasionally as though about to run, then seemed to control the impulse. Back in the cabin, I watched cautiously from behind a drawn curtain. Peter moved without hesitation to the corn, then turned and looked toward the doe, who began to step forward uncertainly. So that movement in the window should not alarm her, I stood perfectly still until she had lowered her head to sample the grain. In the morning, beside the tracks of Peter and the doe, there were fawn tracks, no doubt made by the twins whose tails I had seen going into the brush. Peter had invited company to share his windfall of food.

At midday, Ade spotted the doe in the shadows of the brush. She had a way of standing that was all her own—

front legs spread, head lifted as though she peered through the lower half of bifocals, one ear forward, the other back, so that they gave the effect of one of those rakehell Australian hats. We remembered that stance from the year before. This was Snowboots' mother, with her new fawns.

Just before dusk Peter rounded up the three of them from their retreat in the woods and brought them down into his cedar garden. The doe was nervous about coming so near the cabin in the light but finally followed him, while the two fawns, identifiable in side lighting as little bucks by the tufts of hair on their foreheads, stood on the bank and sniffed the delicious cedar odor. Peter withdrew, leaving the doe alone in his garden. Only when it was almost fully dark did she in some way signal to the fawns, who leaped down to feed beside her.

When Peter returned later the family was gone and with them all the cedar. Peter sniffed around, looking hopefully at the cabin. Ade scraped up a few leaves that remained in the storage building and we filled out Peter's supper with oatmeal, which he liked almost as well as carrots.

With four deer coming for cedar, Ade had to make long treks through the forest for it, so that he would not strip the trees near the house nor damage any tree by too much cutting. He pulled most of the leaves from the cut boughs where they fell so that he could carry a large quantity in a box, but he always brought enough branches to keep Peter's garden looking as it had when the doe and her twins first came. You would not think that wandering through the woods would offer much news, but Ade almost always had something to report, from the moose he glimpsed near a swamp to the geological surveyor who heard the snap of the pruner and took off at high speed. It took us some time to figure out that the sound was similar to that of a bolt-action rifle being cocked.

Peter spent much time roaming his woods these days, but we had fine company in the doe and her children, although she was still doubtful of our intentions and most suspicious of any changes in the yard. As is the case with most wild creatures, she inspired her own name, and became Mama from her devoted care of her fawns, one of whom we called Pig because he ate hugely and was strictly for himself. His twin became Brother as a matter of course.

One morning Ade put out suet and corn while Mama and her little bucks stood at the edge of the woods. Pig immediately rushed in to eat. Brother followed and joined him at a corn pile. Pig slashed out with his front hoofs, striking Brother's cheek and side. Mama crossed the yard in one leap and Pig guiltily jerked back from the corn. She, however, went to Brother, so Pig began to guzzle again.

Mama, after licking Brother's cheek and moving her nose gently along his side as though checking for injury, saw him settled to eat at a corn pile some distance away. Then she approached Pig and bumped him away from the corn with her lowered head. He reared, forefeet ready to strike. Mama, looking as though she could not believe he had shown such disrespect, brought her hoof smartly down on his head. The sound of the blow reminded Ade of his grandmother, who had whacked similarly with her thimble. Pig backed off, shaking his head, then tried to approach the corn again, but Mama blocked his way with raised hoof. He withdrew to the woods' edge and stood watching the other two enjoy their meal.

When they went back to the woods, Mama acted as though Pig did not exist. When he walked toward her, she moved away and bent her head to eat some cedar leaves that lay on the snow. He stood dejectedly by himself, head hanging. Mama's fluttering eyelashes told Ade and me that she was watching him, although from his point of view she seemed to be ignoring his occasional glances. Later she walked toward him as though by chance. He looked up quickly, but let his head droop when she gave no response. Then she faced him, head lifted. He moved toward her step by step, gradually raised his head, and reached his nose out to her. Mama affectionately washed his face.

Restored to his usual high spirits, Pig ran toward the corn, Brother following. Pig, with perfect deer manners, shared a corn pile quietly with Brother. Mama, overseeing them from the edge of the woods, looked as though well satisfied with her exercise in discipline.

Suddenly she tensed, listened, stomped. The fawns joined her and the three stood, ears belled in the direction of the road. A car stopped. The sound sent the deer leaping, white tails lifted, into the shelter of the forest.

It was growing dim inside the cabin so Ade gathered the lamps onto the kitchen table to trim their wicks and top off the oil. Although I love the soft, warm glow of lamplight, I detest washing the chimneys, which seem bent on sliding out of soapy hands to smash and scatter razor-sharp bits of themselves everywhere. So I was polishing the thin glass to a fine shine with newspaper when there came a thunderous knocking.

"I wonder who that is?" I said.

"There's a way to find out," Ade said, flinging open the door.

Esther and George Barnes, who live year-round at their lodge some twenty miles from us, came in with loud shouts of "Merry Christmas! Happy Birthday!"

"A little late for Christmas, isn't it?" I asked, snatching for a parcel Esther was jiggling on one hand while she unzipped her padded red jacket with the other. "And whose birthday?"

"Mine," said George, taking Ade's cap and jacket from their hook on the wall and handing them to him. "Come on with your toboggan. We'll need it to get the sack down the path in this deep snow."

Ade followed him out and Esther tossed her jacket and scarf over a chairback and ruffled up her short dark hair.

"What sack?" I asked of the closing door.

"Oh, Jacques came along your road a while back and saw your buck's tracks," Esther said, "so we brought him a sack of corn for Christmas. Peter, I mean—not Jacques."

"We haven't seen Jacques for a long time. I thought he went to some lumber camp in Canada."

"He did, but not till a month ago. Just after he stopped at our place." Esther looked out the window. "D'you suppose Peter'll come around? I'd like to see him."

"Maybe. I haven't seen him today and the other deer took off when they heard your car stop. Peter's a real beauty."

I put the kettle on.

"You'd think Jacques had reared him from the egg," Esther said.

"He told us how to feed him. We didn't know, and Peter wouldn't still be around otherwise."

"So it's a joint accomplishment." She squealed as my elbow whacked the parcel on the counter. "Be careful of that. It's a cake."

Refraining from saying that she had almost dropped it when she first arrived, I slid the package respectfully to one side. Esther is one of those talented women who can whip up a cake between chores and produce a miracle of flour and eggs and such that outdoes in looks those fancy things in magazine ads. And the eating is better than the looking.

"Wonderful. Do I get a hunk? My birthday isn't too far off."

"This is for all our birthdays—mine's in March and Ade's is in June or July, isn't it? What difference does it make?"

"June," I said, setting out plates and cups and handing her a knife. "You cut it."

And what difference *does* it make, I thought, as I measured tea into the time-darkened silver pot. Here, where the seasons are more important to living than the days, where one thinks of events, Indian-fashion, as happening "the summer of the forest fire in Canada" or "the winter when the ice was five feet thick," where friends live far apart and traveling is difficult, where time is never long enough for the work to be done, any get-together is a celebration.

Ade and George returned to light the lamps, and we carried our plates and cups into the living room, where the red mahogany of the grand piano blended with the pale brown of the spruce-log walls and an old, hand-carved maple daybed nudged the racks of records, which had not been played since we left the city. By light reflected from the yellow panels between the beams that supported the peaked roof, I looked with affection at George's wind-reddened face, at Ade's somewhat whiskery chin, at Esther's relaxed smile and the white-barred slices of her four-layer chocolate cake, even at the tea. And when we had finished the cake and reported progress on my writing and Ade's drawing and the Barneses' plans for a new home, Peter crowned the evening by tapping on the step and receiving a measure of his own Christmas corn.

Esther and George offered to bring more grain, but could not say when because of the pressure of their busy days. As our supply diminished, Ade hauled out a bag of laying food, left over from our chickens-for-eggs days. At first the deer sniffed at this suspiciously; then Pig and Brother tasted it and cleaned it up, even to the crumbs that were buried and had to be eaten along with bites of snow. When this was gone I gave them oatmeal, carefully rationed because it tends to absorb moisture from the deer's mouth and turn into a sticky or frozen mess, depending on the season, if it lies outside too long.

When Esther and George returned, they brought three sacks of grain, a hundred pounds each of cracked corn, whole-grain oats, and scratch feed, which contained wheat, barley, and wild seeds in addition to oats and corn. We put out separated piles of each kind under Peter's tree and in new locations at the edge of the forest where the big trees offered a different kind of cover. The deer showed little preference for one grain over the others, but ate more, especially of the rich corn, on very cold days and when it was snowing heavily. Peter did not concern himself with the new feeding places unless the supply under his tree was gone, but Mama took the twins there at once, seemingly more confident with the forest at her back.

The deer did not gorge as horses will if let into the oats bin but took relatively small portions, considering that their first stomach can hold two gallons or more. Just how much browse they might have eaten before they came for grain I could not know. The second and smaller stomach is another type of storage chamber. Digestion takes place in the last two stomachs. This elaborate arrangement gives deer an advantage in time of danger, when they may hastily eat a large quantity of food, then go into hiding to rest, chew their cud, and digest the food.

Since whitetail deer of numerous species are found over North America south of the Tree Limit, except in the Far West—and one shrinking species is found even there in pockets near the coast of Oregon and Washington—their food varies with the vegetation of their particular habitat. Acorns and apples are favorites in the East and South and, in cultivated areas where the whitetails have multiplied beyond the ability of the remaining wild lands to feed them, fields and truck gardens must be enclosed by deer-proof fences if the crops are to escape premature harvesting. However, in our immediate area I know of only one oak, planted years ago by Esther Barnes, and I have seen only one apple tree, which drops fruit from its generous boughs onto the lawn of a lovely old white house in our nearest village. Farming is not a major occupation in cleared lands here because of the short growing season.

The magnificent forest of red and white pine that greeted Minnesota's early settlers supported moose and woodland caribou on its evergreens and its foliose lichens, but supplied so little food for whitetails that they were unknown along the North Shore of Lake Superior until 1870 and did not appear inland until the great forests were felled, mainly between 1890 and 1920. Deer browse on the cutover land reached a peak between 1910 and the early 1940's, when the last-grown of it began to rise above the deer's reach. Now considerable acreage is being lumbered again and the brush that will spring up to cover the soil will provide good deer food for another twenty years or so.

On our particular lake shore winter deer browse has not been too good for some time. Certain sections of the forest are so old that low growth does not flourish under the shading trees. Nourishing red osier dogwood grows here only in small amounts. The red and mountain maple, which are much browsed in both winter and summer, were, although brushy in form, mostly grown to tree height when we moved here in 1954. Much of this maple is jagged and malformed from deer breaking down branches in winter to get at the nourishing twigs. New growth of these maples, and of the very scarce striped maple, also called moosewood, along our side road and under power lines has been killed by herbicides. Although there must have been seed trees of the striped maple, I have not found any of this species since the spraying. The northern white cedar, a staple for winter browsing, was trimmed up to a height of seven feet by the deer before we arrived and young white cedars were rare, most saplings having been destroyed early in their lives by the deer's feeding.

To the east of the log cabin, just outside the kitchen door, are a number of these cedars, perhaps two hundred years old. Their trunks are not as thick as those of similar age which grow in swampy lands, and the space around them has been cleared so that their branches spread widely, but even here they had been eaten out of reach by deer before we came. When the branches are heavy with rain or snow, they droop, and one must bend double to pass under them without getting a bath or a face wash. Ade originally planned to trim them higher.

Then, when Peter had been with us a couple of months, a heavy snow weighed down the branches and he lifted his head to eat their leaves. The snow dropped off and the branches snapped back to their first position when he released them. Later another snow came under different weather conditions and froze on the branches in heavy clumps. These clung to the limbs so that they stayed down and Peter trimmed them neatly. The snow on the ground packed hard and crusted firmly enough to bear his weight, so that from drifts he was able to feed from still higher branches, formerly far beyond his reach. Except on the day he came, when hunger drove him to attempt it, he never tried to stand on his hind feet and pull down the branches, as Mama did. In the spring a few of the browsed branches died off, but most of them put out new greenery. Ade marked "Trim cedars" off his list of things to do, and deer still feed from their snow-weighted branches.

In forests where hemlock grows, porcupines help the deer through the winter by letting cuttings fall. But we have no hemlock except a few plants of the ground type, also called yew, which are buried by winter snow, and the porcupine has disappeared from most of our great forest, perhaps due to disease, perhaps controlled by fishers. In the porcupine's stead the little red squirrels play an important part in deer feeding, which in turn is affected by the ever-swinging balance of nature.

Our red squirrels feed during winter on the seed-stuffed cones of spruce, balsam fir, pine, and white cedar, and a variety of mushrooms. An infestation of spruce budworms defoliated the spruce and balsam-fir trees during 1958, 1959, and 1960, and the trees were too weakened to produce cones from 1958 through 1963. During the first three of these years the squirrels stored quantities of pine cones, cedar cones, and mushrooms, supplementing these with my corn and graham crackers. In 1961 and 1962 drought caused even these crops to fail. The squirrels begged and stored pounds of crackers, but even so they came daily throughout the winter to beg more food, in spite of going into the cold season fat and in excellent condition from the quantities of budworm pupae they had eaten.

When the spring of 1963 arrived, I had only to step outside to be almost attacked by patchy-looking squirrels —jumping, scratching, clawing, snapping at my hands. One day I heard a pitiful whimper and found a squirrel on the feeding shelf by the door. I held out a cracker and he nibbled at it without raising his head. After eating a little he managed to sit up, but slumped sideways. Finally I held him in my hand to feed him. He seemed to weigh no more than a mouse and, through his sparse coat, I could feel his bones. This was the bitter shape of starvation, not resulting, as in Peter's case, from finding nothing to eat, but from malnutrition in the absence of natural foods. When the sad little creature had gained enough strength to wobble away and sprawl at rest in the sun, I took a sharp look at my stores of food.

I made a thick sauce of flour, dry milk solids, and water, flavored half of it with cheese and half with sweet chocolate, worked in as much vitamin-and-mineral-rich MPF, a multipurpose food designed to sustain human life in emergencies, as the sauce would hold, and spread the mixture a quarter inch thick in flat pans. When it was cold and solid, I cut it into squares and offered them to the squirrels. They sniffed, tasted, ate, and came for more. Three days later they stopped scratching and snapping. After a month on grain and my home-cooked dietary supplement, with assorted insects on the side, their ragged fur was changing to the normal red sleekness of summer, but their poor winter diet had so weakened them that their 1963 matings produced no young. I have little doubt that, in areas where wild crops failed and the squirrels received no help from human neighbors, many perished.

The forest vegetation, recovered from the budworm attack which had destroyed mostly trees previously diseased or insect-damaged, and lush from 1964's plentiful rain, produced a bumper crop. There was no begging at the door in the fall. The squirrels were deep in the woods, hiding pine and balsam cones and mushrooms in private hollows everywhere, zigzagging under cover when they crossed the yard to prevent their trails being followed to their caches. They took few cedar cones.

During the first part of the winter they had black and sticky forepaws and faces from dining on their rosin-covered stores. As the snow grew deeper and their stored cones diminished, they began to cut the bunches of little cedar cones, which look like wooden flowers. Along with this squirrel food, many cedar leaves were nipped off and fell onto the snow. And deer ambled along their trails, stepping aside to lick up the cedar that the squirrels had cut down. Those deer that came to us for grain took considerably less than they did before the squirrels began to harvest the cones from the cedars, and Ade stopped cutting branches because the few he brought down early in the season were untouched.

As I watched the whitetails, I thought how far removed from their well-being seemed a budworm attack on spruce and balsam fir which, though excellent food for moose, are only starvation stuffers for deer. How unlikely it seems, until one thinks it through, that a large population of our little red squirrels in areas of overbrowsed cedar may spell the difference between a fair winter and hunger, even death, for deer. And yet how inevitable it is that any change in a habitat would affect all phases of its interconnected life.

I had thought of such unbalance long before the occurrence of the hungry squirrels, on an evening when Mama, Pig, and Brother finished a meal of corn and cedar and settled on the bank to chew their cuds. Up came the balls of food, plainly visible against the graceful curves of their throats. Out puffed the cheeks as the steady, rhythmic chewing began. Pig usually took too big a "bite," and sent part of each cud back down to temporary storage before he began to chew. Down the throats went the masticated cuds and up came others.

These deer were plump and comfortable; as content, no doubt, as deer may be. But out of our fondness for them, our enjoyment in watching them, our interest in their behavior, Ade and I were contributing to a change in the natural sequence of events in our part of the forest. Were we doing the right thing or were we wrong?

As snow deepens, deer gather in yards, where they pack the snow with their hoofs and so may move about easily. If the browse there is good and the deer's number not too large, they winter well. If too many deer deplete the browse, and if the snow around a depleted yard is too deep, they lunge and struggle, trying to get through. Soon exhaustion and starvation take their pitiful toll. As the deer increase and browse is depleted over large areas, the situation worsens from year to year until mass starvation, followed by regrowth of the browse, brings the deer herds again in line with their food supply.

In this area timber wolves, if they had not been interfered with, would have limited the number of deer and, indirectly, protected the plants that are the deer's food. But when we moved here, northeastern Minnesota had only three to four hundred of these wolves, and this was the largest population left in the United States.

The situation arose from an assortment of causes: a maudlin affection for deer, a reasonless fear or hatred of wolves, a desire for bounty money, a wish for deer to entertain tourists, and a determination to produce deer for hunters, who are widely said to control deer. But deer withdraw to inaccessible places before an influx of hunters, few of whom go very far from conveniences. Wolves will go where men do not, and on a lessening of their persecution depended (and still depends despite the recent veto of Minnesota's bounty law by Governor Rolvaag) the future well-being of the whitetails deep in this forest.

I looked again at the little family lying in the snow, Pig and Brother side by side and a little behind Mama. Gradually the chewing stopped and all three were quiet, the fawns asleep with their heads down, Mama still with her head up and watching. Quietly Peter stepped into the yard, ate a few mouthfuls of cedar, then jumped onto the bank. Mama turned her head toward him and they stared at eash other, motionless, for half a minute. Then Mama lowered her head and closed her eyes, as Peter moved to a hummock and took over the guard duty.

I looked at him and thought once again of when he had come starving from the shadows. It had not been wrong to help him, not for him nor for us, and it would not be wrong as long as we remembered we must help the forest, too.

We faced no immediate population explosion in our yard from one doe and three bucks, but we had the ingredients of unbalance to come. Although our supplementary feeding took pressure from the browse and gave it a better chance to seed and regrow, it encouraged the deer's increase in a small way as the persecution of the wolves did in a large way. To offset the effect of the feeding, we must encourage wild deer browse by cutting tall maple so

that it might spring anew from the roots, by protecting
white cedar sprouts until they grow large enough to survive the deer's feeding.

To give the comfort of enough to eat and the security
of a secluded resting place to animals who would otherwise face hunger and danger all their lives was a small return for what they brought to us.

Late March

I looked at the two-pound coffee can on top of the oil stove. The brown and red and green ice, layer on layer of juices from meat and canned vegetables, had thawed free of the can. I eased the dripping ice into a kettle, set it on the range, and added a quart of hot water and four beef bouillon cubes. I broke an egg (our last until we could get more from town) into a bowl, sprinkled on salt, and worked two cups of flour into the egg with a fork. When the mixed juices were boiling, I added the crumbly contents of the bowl, stirred the mixture, and put on a lid. In ten minutes that kettle would hold some of the best soup you could eat, and its base was odds and ends I should not have thought of saving before we moved to the woods. Even the birds had had their share—the fat skimmed from the chilled meat drippings.

I suppose any marked change of environment brings about a change in one's sense of values, especially so great a reorientation as Ade and I experienced when we left the convenience and services of a crowded city for our self-sustained, isolated cabin. We no longer wasted useful things and we no longer wanted useless things, but our basic interests had not changed. Instead of designing billboards, Ade drew animal illustrations. Instead of writing technical reports, I did nature stories. He pottered with old radios for fun as he had always done, and I still read mysteries, everything from the polite adventures of *The Circular Staircase* to the tense and terror-filled career of Matt Helm.

As I timed the soup, I considered that thing called "escape." Mysteries, I have been told, are escapist literature because "they take you out of yourself." So does an unabridged dictionary if you concentrate while you are using it. Mysteries simply entertain me. Then there were all those friends who, when they learned of our planned move, said in shocked tones, "Escape!" There is something sad about this kind of thing. People cannot escape by running away, because most difficulties in ordinary living arise from inside—and no one can leave himself behind. Ade and I did not run away from Chicago. We still love the blustery, noisy city, but we felt that we could more readily build the kind of life we wanted in the North Woods. We moved toward something, not away from anything—and there is a world of difference.

I looked at the clock and took off the soup, which was to be Ade's lunch when he returned with the mail. I went out and plowed through knee-deep fresh snow to the thermometer. Twenty above zero—and the calendar said spring had arrived the day before! Ade's snowshoes had left a patterned track up the hill. Three miles away, by the mailboxes, he was probably sitting beside a little fire with the Indian girl from across the lake. If the plow had already come up the main road, the mail would be there any time. If not, they were no doubt speculating as to when or whether it would come. With a chocolate bar, a thermos of coffee, dark glasses to protect against the danger of snow blindness, and pleasant company, a long wait was just one of those things that belong to our kind of life.

Down the path, heels flying, rumps bouncing, ears flopping, came Pig and Brother, full of visions of corn. Hastily I put out grain and almost on my heels they jumped in to start eating. Mama stopped on the path, looked at me, and stomped, so I went obediently inside and took my place at the window.

Pig and Brother were now so tall that from the back they looked very much like Mama, who was a small doe. Antler bumps were lifting the tufts of reddish hair on their foreheads. Mama's little bucks were growing up.

Peter walked part way down the path, turned aside to follow a trail through the brush, and reappeared in the cleared area near where Pig and Brother were jumping from grain pile to grain pile and Mama was eating in a more sedate manner. Peter turned toward the road and stood guard, only his ears moving as he followed sounds too faint for human hearing to catch. After the others had made a good start in cleaning up the grain, he turned his head toward them and flipped his ears forward. Mama in turn looked toward him with her ears forward. Ten seconds later Mama tapped Brother lightly on the neck with a hoof and nudged him in the rump with her head. He turned toward her and the long look with ears forward passed between them. Then Brother trotted up to take over the guard duty and Peter came in to feed.

Brother was not as relaxed at the job as Peter had been. His tail twitched and his rump jerked every time he adjusted his ears. He pushed his nose forward and sideways and tested the air with widespread nostrils, listened and watched as though he knew that his life and the lives of others might some day depend on his alertness when he stood guard over a feeding herd.

Mama and Peter kept unobtrusive watch on him and soon Mama went over to lick his nose. Brother returned the lick enthusiastically and covered the short distance back to the feeding area in a series of frisky hops. Mama came back to chew her cud under Peter's tree and Peter nudged Pig up to the guard position.

Pig plainly thought little of this business. He stood with head down, ears lazily moving now and then, and spent more time looking back toward the remaining grain than he did in watching for possible enemies. Then, when Peter and Brother both were turned away from him, he bypassed Mama and slunk quietly back to the grain.

He had taken only one mouthful when Peter spun around and whacked both his front hoofs down on Pig's rump. Pig jerked away, gave a small snort, and took off into the woods. Peter went after him, leaping on a course to cut off the disobedient fawn. Pig had no chance of outdistancing Peter and soon returned, still at a full run, with Peter first beside him, then ahead. At the proper moment, Peter whirled and reared in front of Pig, who skidded to a stop and went down in the snow. Peter, grunting and snorting, shook threatening front hoofs above the cringing Pig, who, crestfallen, rose and took over his neglected guard duty.

Peter and Brother completed their meal and stood by Mama, chewing their cuds. Pig still held his position, now and then glancing hopefully toward the adults. They ignored him, as Mama had ignored him before when he was in need of discipline.

Suddenly his ears flipped up and turned in the direction of the road. His tail switched and his body quivered. Maybe there was something to this guarding business after all! He heard something coming. His ears followed the sound as it approached along the road. Now Peter joined him and added his experience in listening. Mama and Brother stood side by side, ready to run if necessary.

Bushes moved as a little wind wandered across the path from the road. Peter tested the scents it carried, then relaxed and walked back to Mama and Brother. Pig looked puzzled, but stood his ground until Ade came into view, when Mama stomped lightly and Pig rejoined the group, all of whom stood quietly watching until Ade had passed. By the time he was brooming snow from his boots on the doorstep, Pig was finishing his lunch, Mama was guarding, and Peter and Brother had resumed their calm cud chewing.

Ade and I have seen this silent—at least to our ears—communication between deer many times, most often when they were changing guard while feeding or resting, apparently so that all might get a share of the responsibility and the relaxation. At first we thought it was accompanied by stomping, but the closest watching revealed no movement of their feet in this connection. They may make sounds within the range audible to humans but too soft for human ears to hear, or perhaps they may "speak" in frequencies above or below that range. It is even possible that they communicate in some way alien to man. Jacques once asked me if I had ever felt a deer's "startle," explaining that when he was back in the woods he sometimes felt an abrupt uneasiness. If he turned slowly he would usually spot a deer watching him, poised to run. He thought his uneasy feeling was a projection of the deer's alarm at seeing him. I thought he was joking until it happened to me a couple of times when strange deer, moving along the old trail on the hill, saw me in the yard and paused to evaluate the situation. I have no idea what alerted me to their alarm. I only know that I sensed something when none of my ordinary five senses had indicated that any living thing was near me.

Wild deer react to the slightest movement and to any change in a familiar environment, and Mama was the most cautious of all the deer that have come to know us. When she was learning to approach the feed without Peter's encouragement, I stood motionless in the path one day to watch her. She saw me, ducked her head, peered forward, and stomped. She kept this up so long that I finally moved one hand involuntarily and she was off and out of sight in two leaps.

She scouted and investigated every change in the yard —a toboggan leaning against a tree, Ade's snowshoes stuck upright in a drift, a decrease of a few pieces in the size of the woodpile. The day we did a washing in winter and hung it out to freeze dry, Mama merely glimpsed this apparition and fled with her twins, all three blowing. Even Peter, who learned to accept most of our human peculiarities, would not approach a line of clothes, especially when some of the moisture had sublimated and the limp cloth flapped in the wind as though alive. Ade stretched a line across the kitchen and we dried the washing there in installments. This suited the deer and humidified the dry air in the cabin, but running one's face into a wet sheet in the dark adds nothing to a sleepy trip to check on stove or temperature. This led to one of Ade's brightest ideas, for which he gives credit to the deer.

We do our big washings with a gasoline-powered machine. It took up a corner of the already crowded kitchen and was a nightmare to use in winter, when the flexible exhaust pipe had to be pushed outside through a hole in the kitchen door. The engine noise and oil fumes gave me a headache. The hot exhaust pipe always managed to touch the linoleum and scorch it. The water from the wringer sometimes poured onto the floor, instead of back into the machine. The cabin chilled when a drain hose was attached and passed outside through the partially open door. It was better than trying to wash blankets by hand in a dishpan, but far removed from a modern home laundry.

I came in from a walk one day and found Ade wiping dust from the logs in the empty corner where the washing machine had stood. I looked around. He laughed.

"It's out in the woodshed; you walked right by it. From now on we wash outdoors."

"In this weather?"

"Of course not." He was very superior in manner. "As soon as it's warm enough. Meanwhile we do the bare necessities by hand."

And so we do. During the winter we stack the big

things as they become soiled and keep ourselves in clean shirts and sox as the need arises. On the first clear, warm day in spring Ade hauls the machine out of the shed and tends its engine while I sort clothes. Then, with the sun shining on us and the squirrels chattering underfoot, while the fumes fade away on the breeze, we wash, rinse, wring, and hang. Then we shove the machine back into its shelter until the next time. In the fall we sit on the step, breathing in the scent of the dying leaves, following the play of light on the red-and-gold maples, perhaps running to the shore to watch a flock of wild geese wing over, while the gas engine pops and the machine washes everything—curtains, rugs, blankets, clothes. When the snow is down, the deer and the Hoovers no longer have to bother about clothes on a line.

A few days after Pig had been disciplined for neglecting his lesson in guarding, we had one of those heavy, wet March snows whose flakes melt on contact with your clothes and pile up in soggy masses on tree branches. As the sun climbed the temperature rose with it and the woods were full of dull rumblings and thumps as gathering masses poured down from trees and big snowballs dropped from boughs. The deer came unusually early, snatched their grain, and stood restlessly under the trees. There was no lying quietly to chew their cuds and no single guard. All of them were alert and listening, as Peter had been when alone in such weather the year before. Sometimes Mama stomped when she heard a particularly heavy thud, as though she could not be sure other deer were not nearby. The falling snow and Mama's stomping did not sound alike to me and I wondered if the vibration in the earth might not be as important as the sound, or even more so, to the deer. They do communicate by stomping, and I am not surprised that some woodsmen think that the small glands that lie between the central toes that form the deer's hoofs are a kind of ear, with which the deer listen to the stomping. However, these glands secrete a waxy substance which is believed to enable a doe to trace her very young fawn if it should wander away. The large glands inside the hind legs are the important scent glands, but the purpose of the pair of glands on the outside of the lower part of these legs, marked by tufts of white hair, is not known.

The next day the temperature dropped rapidly. This stopped the fall of snow from the trees but started a quick freezing of water that had gathered on the surface of the lake ice. As the new ice thickened, the great strains set up by its expansion caused it to break with noisy booming and sometimes such violence that we could feel the shock wave in the cabin. These vibrations added to the deer's uncertainty and once, after a very heavy tremor, they scattered and ran wildly. It took Peter more than an hour to herd them back into the yard again.

Lights also confuse deer. Once when I turned a flashlight across the yard and its beam was made visible throughout its length by a heavy fog, Pig lifted his head and tried to lick it. When his tongue could not feel what his eyes could see, he bleated and ran. Strong light projected on deer from behind throws shadows in front of them, which move as the deer sway. Their ears and noses tell them nothing is there, but their eyes contradict this. I have seen similarly confused hares nibbling at the edge of a spot of light, and those flying squirrels who will take food from my hand sometimes try to bite the shadow of a cracker instead of the cracker itself. These and probably other wild creatures simply do not understand beams of light.

If I turned my flashlight into the forest shadows, I often saw the deer's eyes, blazing like drops of molten gold, bobbing and swaying as the animals froze and faced the blinding brightness. In less brilliant light their eyes may look orange or pink or yellow-green, and, when a light strikes them from the side, a person looking from behind the light source may see an eye that looks red or green.

Outlaw hunters make use of this vulnerability of deer. They travel back roads, picking up the deer's eyes in their headlights or by means of spotlights or powerful flashlights. The last are sometimes used to locate deer when they come to lakes or streams to drink. This is called jacklighting or shining. Spots of light in blackness are a poor target and an uncertain one because the eyes of other animals from bears to cows also shine in direct light. A bear will often blink every second or so as he stares into light, but cows' eyes look like those of deer. Probably many animals shot by such poachers run away to die. They cannot be followed by night and the poacher, having shattered the silence with his shot, would not be inclined to stay long in the immediate area anyway.

In an attempt to reduce the number of night deer kills on highways, experiments have been made with mirrors, set to reflect headlight beams back from the road's edge, in the hope that the reflections might strike the eyes of deer about to cross and hold them back until the car has passed.

This has not been generally successful, although in places where deer follow well-worn trails reflections directed along those trails might help.

A "Deer Crossing" sign by a highway means "Slow down! Watch the roadside!" especially in spring and fall. Kills in the spring are often more unfortunate because the does, heavy with fawn, are very vulnerable and a dead pregnant doe usually means three lives gone. When one deer crosses a road, other adults may follow, and after the fawns arrive they will follow their mother.

A deer may run in panic ahead of a car on a narrow road, trying fruitlessly to scramble up high banks of earth or snow that wall in the right-of-way. If the driver will stop, the deer will usually stop also. Once it realizes that the car is no longer following, it will leap with ease and grace from one side of the road across and up to safety on the opposite bank. A deer needs room to make those beautiful leaps that are its means of escape from danger.

In April of 1964, Ade and I drove to Duluth. (Yes, we had a car by then.) On the way down along the shore of Lake Superior, eleven deer leaped across in front of us and six lay dead beside the road. We came back at dusk when the deer were beginning to move more freely than in the daytime. Small groups stood by the road, wanting to cross to get water, but hesitating and uncertain. We stopped for them and the majority crossed at once. As it grew dark, to the moving bright lights of the cars was added the intermittent glare of those reflecting highway signs that can blind even the drivers. The deer seemed to bolt at random, unable to tell whether the lights were stationary or moving. It took us three times as long to cover this stretch of road as it had going the other way in the morning, but we did not add to the toll of highway-killed deer, nor wreck our car and endanger our lives in the process. In 1963 game wardens received reports of 2,399 deer killed on Minnesota highways by cars, some of which were badly damaged and their occupants seriously injured. A little less hurry, a little more patience—that is a small price for a safe journey.

But in the days when Peter and Mama were educating Pig and Brother before our eyes, we gave little thought to having no transportation except our feet. There was more than enough to entertain us in sight of the windows, and we spent many hours learning to know the four deer as individuals. Their temperaments varied as do those of humans, and each had his own ways of doing things.

Peter, from his second day with us, always indicated that he wanted something to eat by tapping on the step with a front hoof. When he wore his antlers, they usually knocked against the door, but I think this happened accidentally when he poked his head forward to look inside through the glass panel.

Mama's method was to stand some fifteen feet from the door and stare fixedly at it, ears forward, as she did when she seemed to be communicating with another deer. If we did not bring out feed, she went around the cabin, looked from window to window until she saw us, then again took up her ears-forward stance. We checked frequently to see if the deer needed food, so Mama may have thought that her system worked. One night, however, we heard such a snorting and stomping by the door you would think that the deer had been beset by a dozen feral dogs. We rushed out to see Mama, ears forward, eyes fixed on the door, and apparently at the end of her patience. In the morning we saw from her tracks that she had made three circuits of the cabin, stopping each time around to stare into every window!

Pig was more direct and nosed at the glassed-in flower-box Ade had built in the living-room window. He could see us, and we could see him and supply his grain at once.

Brother, usually retiring, began near the end of January to stand outside the window by the table where I wrote. He did this when there was plenty of corn, and I decided that he was merely curious, possibly attracted by the sound of the typewriter. But he sometimes came when I was not typing and when I was not even at the table, so I planned a sort of survey, hoping to learn what interested him.

I started by checking the grain whenever he came. He always followed me to look at it, but returned immediately to the window. Whatever prompted him to his long waiting had to do with food, but I did not understand what it was. Then, in mid-March, we ran low on corn and eked it out with oatmeal. Brother dashed at the oatmeal pile as though it were for his delight alone. I soon saw that he came to the window only when there was no oatmeal. If I went out and gave him some, he ate it and bounded away. If I went out and did not leave any, he checked and returned to the window. Remembering the flavor of oatmeal from our emergency feeding two months before, he had patiently and persistently "asked" for it every day! This cereal has been our treat for deer ever since.

Difficult and slow as it is to understand so simple a thing as a deer's indicating that he wants a special kind of food, it is even more difficult to try to communicate, human to deer. Peter always turned at the sound of his name, possibly because he had been conditioned to it when I used it to help him adjust to his impaired sight by turning his head. Although deer reared as pets may answer to names, none of our wild ones except Peter paid the slightest attention to any particular human words, but if they were alerted by some unusual noise or sight that we knew to be harmless we could sometimes stop them from bolting by whistling or speaking softly. Ade and I customarily keep our voices down outside in this land where there is rarely a need to shout, so we will never know how these deer might have reacted to noisy human speech if they were exposed to it frequently.

Near the end of March on one of those thrilling days when spring is in the air although the ground is still white, Ade and I heard Mama making a great fuss. We went out to see her standing just below the bank, on which her big fawns huddled uneasily together. Mama looked toward us and quieted. We saw nothing out of the way, but when we turned to go in she began again to snort and blow and stomp. I walked slowly toward her and she grew even more excited, finally striking violently at the ground with both forefeet and bleating. I stopped. Mama was evidently trying to tell me there was danger. But what was she so afraid of?

Ade spoke softly from the door.

"You're right beside the henhouse. I put the screen

door in there today. Remember how Bedelia startled Peter?"

So that was it. From the corner of my eye I could just glimpse Bedelia, moving back and forth in her screened doorway and pretty excited herself by all these goings-on. Mama was quiet but tense, watching me closely. How could I tell her there was no danger? When she was uncertain about anything, she stalked it. Feeling a little silly, I decided to stalk the henhouse.

I backed up and made a wide circle behind it, then cautiously approached from the far side, leaned forward and down, and stared at Bedelia—who stared back. Then I straightened up, relaxed, and walked in front of the coop as though it were completely unimportant. When I was back at my first position, I looked at Mama, who still watched tensely.

She turned and looked at the fawns, then moved in her own wide circle until she, too, approached obliquely and peered into the coop. I don't know what might have happened if Bedelia had flapped her wings or cackled, but she merely returned Mama's scrutiny.

Mama went back to her position below the bank, faced the henhouse, and stomped twice, quickly and lightly, the first tap with her right forefoot, the second with her left. The fawns leaped from the bank, one on each side of her, and headed straight past Bedelia to the grain, with Mama following more slowly.

This is the only incident in which I have been able definitely to connect a communicating stomp pattern with a subsequent action. A short time later, I read *Arctic Wild* and learned that Lois Crisler had used a method similar to mine to reassure a frightened wolf. Only then did I feel confident that I had managed to communicate with Mama by imitating deer behavior.

It is a human trait to expect animals to understand people, but it is absurd to even hope for this unless people first try to understand animals.

Late April to June 1

It has been truly said that the first step toward success in the writing game is to apply the seat of the pants to the seat of a chair in front of a typewriter. Perhaps, in life's ordinary circumstances, there are places and times where this is harder to do than in the North Woods in April, but I doubt it.

On an afternoon some four weeks after Mama had been introduced to Bedelia I sat in the prescribed place, trying to concentrate on writing words to cover the blank sheet of paper before me. Just outside my window the fat purple elder buds were unfurling the slim green tips of their leaves. I walked to the west window to see how the willow pussies were doing; they were almost ready to turn into flowering catkins. The patch of bare duff under the big pine, golden-brown with fallen needles, was larger than it had been the day before, and something near its border of withdrawing snow showed fresh and green. I looked back

at the typewriter. It really would only take a minute or two to see what the green was.

As I jumped from bare spot to bare spot, avoiding the glistening heaps of soggy snow and the icy pools of water, the soft breeze soothed my skin and brought me the scent of the warming earth. I came to the little patch of green, made up of tough grass and the scallop-edged leaves of the naked miterwort. Every year I see them, the first green from under the snow, and always they bring me a feeling of beholding a miracle.

Beside them, at the edge of the drainage ditch that here grew shallow as it led away down to a forested slope, I looked at the blackened masses of hairy corms and fallen fronds from which the fuzzy, silvergreen fiddleheads of the interrupted ferns would soon rise. In the silted ditch bottom, trickles of water were converging from under patches of melting ice. As I watched, the trickles united to form an inch-wide stream, hurrying along and cutting a tiny channel in the silt. The little stream divided to encircle a stone, turning it into a pygmy island. I was seeing in miniature the process by which the rivers had changed the land when they flowed from under the melting glaciers ten thousand years before.

I remembered the chair waiting in front of the type-writer and had almost reached the cabin door when I heard a metallic *tink-tink-tink* from the little pile of bare cedar branches under Peter's tree. Three Harris's sparrows, wearing the striking black bibs, masks, and caps of their breeding plumage, had stopped for a rest and some food on their way to far-north nesting grounds and were sounding a vigorous alarm. A red squirrel took it up and two blue jays added their screams.

An ermine was weaving in and around the remaining humps of snow. Ignoring the noisy, offended creatures, he moved away like a blowing feather, his half-molted coat, now brown along the back but still white on the sides, making him seem to appear and disappear as he passed across the motley of snow and earth.

As I looked up at the evergreens moving gently against the azure sky and wondered if I really saw the faintest misting of mauve buds on the top of the tallest birch, Pig leaped high across the path, lightly, as though sailing on the air, with Brother following. They glided, curved, circled, raced, with first one, then the other leading. They flashed across the yard in front of me, their leaps so long and effortless that their hoofs seemed hardly to skim the ground. They cleared a brush pile as though riding a wave. They flowed like liquid, soared like winged creatures, seemed to hover in mid-leap as their lithe young bodies stretched through the exciting air of spring.

At last they drifted down from the bank to drink of the sweet water oozing from the mossy rocks in the ditch's side. They were tall now, almost as tall as Peter, who had stepped out of the woods and was watching them from the bank. They leaped up beside him. When Peter trotted back into the forest, back straight and head high, Pig and Brother trailed him in single file, their backs as straight, their heads as proudly lifted as his.

As the bucks passed out of sight, Mama walked across the yard, flipped easily over a four-foot chicken-wire fence into what was once a garden, and munched some dried grass, released from under the snow. I am still not quite used to the ease with which a deer can clear a fence or other obstacle, perhaps seven or eight feet high. Earlier in the winter I had been standing in the road, Peter a short distance ahead of me and about to cross, when a car roared over a blind hilltop as though the driver could see where he was going. I had a moment of horror—then Peter cleared car, road, and far bank as though he had been shot from a bow. His leap was more than thirty feet long with a rise of at least six feet.

Through with eating grass, Mama flipped back out of the garden as though she were not already growing heavy with her unborn fawns, and hurried to the corn in an awkward, paunch-swaying trot. Even without fawns, she was too low-slung for trotting, but she made up for this lapse from gracefulness by returning to the garden spot using another gait, which I have never been able to figure out, but which is light and complicated like a show horse's dancing step. She had almost reached the fence when a snowshoe hare started up under her feet. She bolted straight into the wire, pulling down posts and generally entangling herself. I was afraid that one of the posts might have struck her abdomen and injured her or her fawns, but she soon shook herself free and, snorting derisively at the vanquished fence, marched into the woods.

On the doorstep I met Ade, fastening his jacket as he came out.

"That does it," he said. "I'm going to pull down what's left of those fences before somebody breaks a neck. I'll use the wire to make Bedelia a better run."

In the beginning the fences had kept hares out of our garden plots. Then Gregory, our first groundhog, found that he could wriggle through the mesh. We saved part of

the garden and turned over the damaged bed to Gregory. The flimsy wire was inconspicuous, almost invisible at dusk, and after the deer had blundered against it several times, I had the supposedly bright idea of tying white cloth strips on it. Pig tried to eat the rags. Then one night the previous fall I heard a terrible roaring and thumping. I peeked out of the partially open door to see a bull moose threshing around with wire and broken posts flying in wide circles from his antlers. One glance was enough. I ducked back inside. In the morning that particular fence looked as though it might have been sat on by an elephant. It was with real pleasure that I watched Ade tearing out the remains of the last chicken wire.

As the four deer began to browse separately I had to look sharp to tell which one might be standing at the edge of the sunlight. Although their winter coats were all a gray tone, variously shaded with blue or brown, their individual markings differed. When their markings were obscured, as they were when their fur fluffed up like coarse plush on very cold days, I watched for differences in stance and little tricks of behavior.

To me, deer look smaller when they are near than they do from a distance, so size does not help me much in identifying individuals who are alone. The species I know so well is the largest of the whitetails, yet they average only around three feet high or a little more at the shoulder. They seem to shrink when they forage with their noses to the ground, and a big buck may not only be taller than the rest of a herd but he towers when he lifts his antler-crowned head.

Mama's fawn of the previous year, Snowboots, was unlike any other deer that I have seen. The nearest thing to his white front stockings was a little whiteness on the front of the feet of a doe Ade and I saw some miles from our cabin. Snowboots was perhaps slightly affected by the genes which cause the dark-spotted white coats of piebald deer, found in the East but which I have never heard of in this area. One of my magazine editors once wrote me that an albino fawn had come to feed in the meadow near his home in Connecticut. These white deer may have defective hearing, as is often the case with albino mink and blue-eyed white kittens. However, an albino squirrel who spent a year or two in our yard seemed to have normal hearing, joining in with the blue jays when they sounded an alarm and responding to the chattering of other squirrels. True albino whitetails are rare, as are black, or melanistic, individuals.

When Pig and Brother were about six months old, they looked much alike. Both had the young animal's cute, short face, with the brow curving down to the muzzle. Their thick, warm coats were the same brownish-gray. Their fine, wide tails were brownish at the top, black about a third of the way up from the tip, and rimmed with white. Both had strongly marked white spots at each side of the upper lip which, when their mouths were closed, joined with the white of the lower lip and gave them the appearance of having fangs. But Brother had a little black toothbrush of a mane halfway up the back of his neck and Pig did not. I was also sure that the maneless fawn was Pig because of his rush to get at the food and his aversion to discipline.

By the time they were a year old and losing their baby-ish appearance, their faces began to differ. Pig's eyelids were white and long, with a dark line above, slanting up and away from the bridge of his nose. This gave him a calculating expression, which was deepened when he laid back his ears like a donkey as he poked his nose into things new and strange. I think his curiosity overcame his sense of caution. Brother's face was slightly paler, and his gentle expression matched his reserved and quiet manner. He had less white on his eyelids than Pig and no noticeable "eye-brow" lines. Both had unusually long protective hairs below their eyes and prominent sparse whiskers extending down and sideways from the front part of the lower jaw. (All deer have these hairs, which are pale in color and can-not be seen at a distance unless highlighted.) Both had ears with rounded tips and an inside rim like black-velvet pip-ing, outlining the fuzzy white winter lining.

All Mama's fawns, and Mama herself, had ears like this. Her coat was very dark gray and the scent glands inside her hind legs were the longest I have seen. She was sway-backed and her paunch sagged, perhaps from carrying fawns, because she was not a young doe when she came to us. Her wide muzzle and her hoofs always looked as though freshly blackened and polished, and this was em-phasized by a narrow band of white just above her nostrils and by paler gray hairs above her hoofs. Her large and liquid eyes were ringed with black as though penciled, and her eyelashes were so long that they looked false. There were strong white eyelid patches which extended well for-ward, and her brow lines, though faint, were clearly marked. With her lovely face, her extreme ear positions, her manner of holding her head high and forward, and her forceful way of maintaining her role as leader of other does in later years, she was unmistakable.

Peter's nicked hoof, blind eye, and notched ear set him uniquely apart. He was the largest buck we have ever seen, and had a gray winter coat, with a prominent brush of black hair on his chest. His ears had somewhat pointed tips, no sign of a black rim, and a dark V-mark in their white lining. This is not uncommon in whitetails but we have not seen it in other deer in our yard. His eyelids were white, and there were slight whitish shadings beneath his eyes. The white band above his nostrils peaked in the center. Even without all this, his very dignified, yet gentle and trusting ways would have set him apart.

As the days warmed and lengthened in May Peter roamed alone. The two young bucks tried to stay with Mama, but she, after licking their noses, struck at them with her front feet, making it plain that it was time for them to begin independent lives. Only occasionally did the four come together in the late afternoon to eat their portion of grain.

Their ears began to lose their cottony lining and their tails became thinner and narrower. They carried their tails tucked close to the body for warmth in winter but let them hang down in warm weather, except in mosquito and fly time, when the tails were used alternately as switches and tucked-in protectors. The winter thickness and length showed best when possible danger threatened and, preparatory to running with flag up, the white edging hairs spread so that the tail covered almost the whole rump.

Their winter coats were beginning to look rough and

straggly and I found bunches of hair lying about the yard. These winter deer hairs are really hollow bristles, air-filled and crinkled to make them excellent insulation against the cold. They are white throughout most of their two- to three-inch length and carry color at the sharply pointed tip.

Pig seemed to be very much irritated by his loose bristles and licked and yanked with his mouth until he soon resembled a patchwork of smooth russet and bushy gray. Brother lost the bristles on his face and brow so that his red summer head with its antler bumps looked out as though from a high-collared gray fur coat. Mama grew uniformly patchy and I had high hopes of seeing how Peter looked during the summer but, before he started to shed, he was gone. I shall always wonder what secluded green place was his during the time when our forest lost its silence and became a vacationland.

In mid-May we woke to find the ice broken out of the lake and the water sparkling blue in the sun. Transparent, melting shells of ice, edged with slim, short icicles balled at the end like bobble fringe, still covered the rocks along the shore. The forest floor was mottled with green growth, brown duff, gray bark and twigs, with scattered gray-white snow remnants, lying in nooks sheltered from the warm south winds and the pattering spring rains.

Mama and the young bucks had plenty of fresh maple shoots, elder leaves, and ground plants to eat now. They took only a little of the grain that we put at the edge of the forest where there was thick brush for cover. Against the background of the maple's new red stems and the earth-and-leaf-patterned ground, the deer's red-and-gray-mixed coats were almost a perfect camouflage. I had to look closely to see them in the dusk, even when I watched from an open window only twenty feet from them, and sometimes I did not locate them until they moved.

Ade and I marvel at the way a deer can be in plain view one minute and, in the blink of an eye, disappear. In the winter their gray coats match the dry stems and the gray snow shadows. In the summer their red coats blend with the color of the red-brown duff. These effects are strengthened by the shading from their dark backs to their white bellies. This counter-shading is important to relatively defenseless creatures, especially small animals like mice. When strong light brightens their backs, heavy shadow falls beneath them and the lightening of the back and the darkening of the belly tend to make their outlines less conspicuous. Powerful mammals like black bears can get along nicely without this protection. In addition to these camouflaging effects, the deer's slim lower limbs are hard to discern among the slender stems of the brush in which they so often feed, and their bodies are so narrow across the rump and shoulders that they may step behind a not very large tree and be instantly hidden.

One evening I searched the shadowy brush for a long time before I was sure there were no deer there. Ade and I kept a careful check on the amount of corn eaten and, near the end of the month, knew that only one deer still came to feed, and that one in the wee hours of the morning. When for three nights the corn decreased by only the small amounts eaten by hares and mice we decided that the last deer was gone for the summer, and reduced the amount of feed so that none would be left to ferment in the warm dampness.

Then on the evening of June first I heard a stomp and the whish of a deer's blowing. Mama stood at the edge of the forest, looking from me in the window to the ground where she was used to finding her heap of corn. Her silky summer coat was not red or bronze but so light it was almost strawberry blonde. Soft gray markings gave her face new and gentler beauty. If it had not been for her mannerisms and her familiarity with the feeding place, I might have been doubtful of her identity. When I brought out some oatmeal and corn, she retreated into the deep shadows, moving slowly and heavily, for her fawns would soon be born.

She had finished eating when the rays of the setting sun fanned through the trees to silhouette her. Her ears were translucent pink in the light and her outline was picked out with gold. She stood quietly chewing her cud until the long twilight began to fade from the northwest. Then, with a flip of her tail, she vanished along the trail she, and perhaps her mother before her, had marked out with shining black hoofs.

the
third
year

THE
FAMILY

June 3 to
Mid-September

As the days warmed, Ade and I had gone back and forth, periodically changing sides, on the question of whether it would be worthwhile to plant a vegetable garden. The earlier ones had done well enough, if one considered the soil and discounted the bed taken over by our groundhog, but they would have failed miserably if we had not hauled uncounted buckets of water uphill from the lake—and there was a long-range prediction of another dry summer. We could foil Gregory by replacing our recently removed fences with something heavier, but to fence in all the beds in this way would surely cost more than the worth of any vegetables we might grow. Then again Gregory might not return, fresh garden peas were delicious, and how about carrots for Peter?

On June third a vigorous scratching on the screen door decided the matter for us. Ade opened the door and Gregory strolled in, standing up to peer cautiously around at every third step. With a handful of molasses cookies, Ade sat down on a chair by the kitchen table. Gregory went to him at once and demolished the cookies systematically, standing up and clawing at Ade's pants legs to ask for more after he finished each one. For dessert Ade offered a saucer of canned sliced peaches. Gregory held the slippery fruit tightly between his hands and, with much slurping and spilling of juice down his fur, ate all the peaches before he put both forepaws into the dish and licked up the syrup. Then, without a backward glance, he turned and marched out the open door, leaving a trail of sticky paw prints. We watched him making a furious assault on the young dandelions and Ade, with what I am sure was a sigh of relief, said: "No garden."

The next day I discovered that Gregory had a taste for daisy leaves and simultaneously saw sprouts from painted daisies that I had thought long gone from deep frost. Getting any kind of tame flower to establish itself in this climate is a major accomplishment, so I called Ade, who was checking the foundation concrete for possible cracks opened by the winter's extremes of temperature and frost.

"See?" I said, pointing to the row of small leaves.

"See what?"

"My daisies."

"Oh. What about 'em? We've daisies all over the clearing."

"But they're *painted* daisies!" This obviously meant nothing to a man whose thoughts of paint in spring ran to walls. "I planted them. They're colored."

"What color?"

"They didn't bloom the first year. Pink, red—who

cares?" I said, smothering a desire to stamp on his toe to
see if he were awake. "I mean they need a fence."

"Those things?" He could not have sounded more incredulous if I had suggested a cage for moonbeams.

"Yes," I said with great firmness. "I'll go in and order
something that will stop Gregory and that the deer can
see." It was hard not to look back to see how he was taking
this. After all, only a month earlier he had been tearing
down fences.

A roll of plainly visible welded wire fabric, with considerable stiffness and a one-by-two-inch mesh, arrived on
the freight truck the next week. Ade took to it at once,
mainly I think because he saw in the accurate separations
of the wires a convenient way to read snow depth at a
glance. He enclosed the small daisy bed and a triangular
bit of ground rich with wild flowers, then built a neat cage
to hold my begonias, previously always losing their best
clusters of pink blooms when squirrels jumped among them
and snapped their brittle stems. Some of the fencing was
left, so I set out to look for white pine seedlings, which
are scarce and fragile and are often destroyed by hares and
deer.

Beneath the great pine that overlooks the cabin and
clearing I found a foot-tall sapling, with three annual rows
of little branches, delicate light-green needles, and promis-
ing buds. It needed protection, not only from being eaten
but from being crowded out of life by the grasses, ferns,
and horsetails that were surging upward from the warm
June earth. I weeded around the small tree and was mulch-
ing the circle of bare earth with fallen pine needles when
I heard a snort from the forest's edge.

Mama, head down, blowing and stomping, blocked the path into the woods. I backed away because she seemed in a fighting mood and I had no wish to come afoul of her striking front hoofs. As I retreated she quieted, and with a last look as though to make sure that I was not going to follow she turned away. I saw that the soft white fur under her tail was damp, her small udder was swollen, and she was no longer heavy with her fawns. Somewhere within the patch of woods between our cabins, in one of those tiny glades so hidden by surrounding vegetation that you can pass straight by without seeing inside, she had given birth to her twins only a short time before.

Ade fenced in the little pine as quietly as possible and, because we thought Mama had come for grain to help quickly restore her energies, put salted corn near the place where she had warned us from the path. We longed to see the little ones but gave first consideration to Mama's instinct to protect her young. When we had reason to go to the summer house, we bypassed our route through the woods by walking up the steep path from the log cabin to the road, following that to the gate next door, and going down another path to the house. Apparently this roundabout way was fine with Mama, as she made no attempt to interfere.

She came in the late afternoon to feed and, after a few days of surveying the new fences from a distance, came out of the brush to eat heartily of our bluebead lilies, which were about to bloom. She never moved far from cover, though, and started a private war with a little red fox who found our yard a good mousing place. She had paid no attention to foxes before, but she probably felt this one was a danger to her fawns. Several times we saw the fox flashing across the yard, tail out and black-velvet feet flying as he dived for cover just ahead of Mama's pounding hoofs. Then she began to watch his trails. One day she circled ahead of him and, when he passed in front of her, leaped up and out, to come down with great force on her four bunched hoofs. The fox yelped and fled, alive by the very hairs of his tail, and did not return.

Although weather is still uncertain in June and the mosquitoes and black flies are at their biting best, people were coming back to the woods, and the movement of wildlife was changing as noticeably as the leaves were filling in the spaces between the boughs.

One morning a yearling black bear came from the woods into the yard. He weighed perhaps a hundred thirty pounds, was around seventeen months old, and was on his own in the forest for the first time. He sniffed and listened and watched for danger. After looking at the cabin for a long time, he bent down a willow sapling and licked off its catkins for a snack, then ambled away in his lazy-looking but ground-covering walk.

He came to a lodge and made his way to a screened window through which drifted delicious odors. As he felt around the window frame his claws hooked under the edge of the screen, and he lifted it out and set it on the ground. Then he climbed inside.

He ate the remains of a coffee cake, left on a table by vacationers in a hurry to go fishing. He pawed around the refrigerator and jumped back when he accidentally depressed the latch and the door swung open. Then he removed a dozen eggs in a carton and set them on the floor without breaking them. He put some pork chops beside the eggs and ate some butter and sausage. He looked into the vegetable bin, but found the potatoes uninteresting. He removed the lid from a garbage can and spread its contents on a sofa, so that he could pick out bread and meat scraps and leave banana peelings and cooked fish heads. He licked bacon grease from a can on the stove and in the next room found an apple which he picked up in his mouth to take with him.

The next day he found the window closed, but another apple lay outside the cabin door. Encouraged, he looked further and found a ladyfinger on the big step in front of the lodge. Still cautious, he loped into the woods with his cake.

As time passed, the little bear lost all fear of people and stood patiently while tourists took his picture. He learned to climb a pole for food and to sit up and flap his paws as zoo bears do, and even to walk a few steps on his hind legs. And when he had performed and eaten and posed, he stretched out on the step in front of the lodge to sleep in deep content, warmed by the sun and secure in his trust.

He roamed regularly along our shore and no doubt was responsible for certain unexplained blowings from Mama. In spite of bears' fondness for insects and berries, they are carnivores, and young fawns would be a fine meal for them. They do not have much chance of catching deer large enough to run, although they can cover ground much faster than you would think watching one ambling along and looking for grubs in stumps. Occasionally, I have been told, they catch a deer in water deep enough to permit pushing it under and drowning it. But Mama seemed less annoyed at the presence of the bear than at that of the fox, or so we thought.

One evening Ade and I were reading when there was a noisy scrabbling up one corner of the cabin, followed by loud thumps on the roof. When quiet was restored, we looked out the door. The little bear was sitting on a tree limb by the woodshed, apparently hoping to catch a flying squirrel when it came for food. The noise had resulted when he chased one of them across the roof, an overly ambitious try considering their split-second movements.

An hour later the full moon flooded the yard with brightness. No flying squirrel would venture out in such light even if there were not a bear near, but the little black fellow was still waiting on the branch. This time I threw a light on him, and he looked down, saying, "Whah? Whah?" I walked away from the cabin to gaze at the pine tops against the cobalt sky and felt a gentle nudge. The bear had slid down the tree to follow me and was walking beside me like a dog, nosing my hand. He wanted something to eat, but I would not feed him or any other bear. I slid my fingers into the thick hair behind an ear and scratched. He liked this and sat down to be petted.

Then Mama stepped into the open some fifty feet from us, upwind and so perfectly relaxed that I felt sure she had not smelled the bear. She looked in our direction, then whirled to face us and stared, ears wide and head forward. She did not move until I lifted my hand from the bear's fur and he stood up. Then she woke the night with a flurry of snorts and stomps and blowing. When neither bear nor human did more than look at her, she leaped into the forest, her blowing growing fainter as she ran. I did not see her again that summer.

However, she had abandoned her nursery prematurely, because later in the day when the little bear was walking through the woods he heard a loud noise and felt a blow. He fell down and could not get up. His chest filled with pain and his mouth with blood, and terror closed over him like ice. There were two more loud noises, but he heard only the first of them—for the second bullet broke his neck.

He had been "eliminated," a common precautionary ending for tame bears. In the beginning no one had intended to bring harm to this friendly young animal, and he had done no harm, but bears, even small ones, are very powerful. When they lose their instinctive fear of man they may be both dangerous to people and destructive of property. This is true not only if they are hungry, angered, hurt, teased, or frightened, but even if they are encouraged to play. One cannot expect them to control their strength.

Every time I go outside, I pass the claw marks the little black bear left on the cedar bole as he slid down to join me in the yard. I remember the thickness of his fur under my fingers, and I wish that no one had fed him, that he had never learned to like people, that he still might be roaming the hills where the blueberries grow.

The summer was dry, sunny, warm, and filled with unexpected visitors. Ade and I developed a regular guided tour—of the lake by boat and of our houses and grounds on foot. It was great fun, and as I look back on it the most surprising thing was that most of our guests were sure they knew exactly how we should remodel not only the cabins but the surroundings. If I showed visitors a small room in a suburban house and said: "This will be our storage room," they would not think of saying: "Oh, no! By all means make it a powder room." Here they did not hesitate to plan everything for us, from a split-level ranch-type house to entirely cleared grounds made into a golf-course-size lawn. I finally gave up trying to explain that our purpose in getting this particular land was to enjoy it and study it in its natural state. I simply said: "How clever. What an unusual idea!" and kept my eye on the terrain that suits me as it is.

In June I had gone out to pick dandelion greens, our favorite spring tonic for both the taste and the flesh. I found almost none. I kept watching for them as I showed our friends around and finally realized that we would not have either our greens or the transient flood of golden flowers. The chipmunks missed them too, standing in the grass and pulling down blades and stems of various kinds, only to let them go when they found no fuzzy ball of seeds at the top. There were many small dandelion plants at the edges of our paths and in the tall grasses, but they made no progress. The field daisies, usually scattered as gaily and thickly as confetti, put forth only a few short-stemmed flowers, their petals so stubby that the blooms looked like small yellow nosegays with plaited white-paper rims. On the other hand, the pink and red and white bouquets of sweet Williams, the white sprays of yarrow, and the purple torches of wild asters flourished in their turns. Gregory's selective liking for dandelion and daisy greens had changed the whole clearing's appearance.

Almost before I was used to the warm weather, September had come and the summer residents were talking about winter plans. Gregory, who had been missing for a week, probably digging out his burrow and putting in a soft bed for winter sleeping, came for an afternoon snack. He ate two molasses cookies, yawning prodigiously between bites, then flopped face down on the sunny path for a rest. His melanistic coat was heavy and shining, almost black on his back and head. His rusty-red sleeves and vest were deep-piled, like plush. Even his inky gloves and sox and his flat tail were more heavily furred than in summer. When he dragged his fat self away, still yawning, he looked fit to stand anything the coldest and longest winter might bring.

Anything that is as strongly suggestive of the oncoming winter as a groundhog's retirement is sure to remind me of the winter grocery order. I settled down with a wholesale catalog and made up a list—cases of vegetables and fruits and meats and spreads, sacks of flour and potatoes and sugar, a whole cheese, a slab of bacon. Then, knowing that I tend to go wild with a grocery catalog and that I must consider both cost and our limited storage space, I blue-penciled my tentative selections, cutting out the unessential, the very expensive, and the overly bulky. I was pleased with the final result: a list that would give us a daily can of fruit or vegetables, enough canned meat for times when we did not have any more of the fresh meat mailed to us by the butcher in town, plenty of material for baking, and even some luxuries. Then I remembered food for the wild creatures. I slashed out the costly crab meat and whole figs and substituted oatmeal, graham crackers, cracked corn, and scratch feed. The whole grocery-order-ing process, sandwiched between this and that, had taken almost two weeks.

Feeling both noble and tired, I waved Ade off to the mail with the order and check in his packsack, and looked at the straw-colored fronds of the ferns and the faintly rosy maple leaves. Beside the paths, where the sun reached brightly even as fall came on, I saw the yellow pompons of dandelions. Now that Gregory had gone, the tough, deep-rooted plants were hastily preparing their seeds.

As I stood in the sun remembering that the average killing frost date here is September twentieth, a snowshoe hare leaped from the forest and passed within two feet of me without paying any attention to me. As I noted that his feet were white, the first change toward his snow-matching coat, I saw hares everywhere, moving in leisurely bounds from the woods between the houses, crossing the clearing and vanishing into the woods to the east. I counted twenty-two, and I am sure I did not see them all because they spread in an irregular line from the lake shore to the road and possibly beyond, some of them moving through thickly leaved brush. Some were big, old grandfathers, others were middle-sized, and a few were dainty and small, from the summer's last-born young. Why they were moving, where they went, I shall never know, but wherever they came from, they had had a strong effect on the vegetation. I thought of Peter, Mama and her fawns, and went into the woods to see how our deer food looked.

I crossed the springy, sun-dappled brown duff under the big trees, where fantastic mushrooms lifted umbrella tops—some as large as dinner plates—of scarlet and pale green, violet-tinged white and chestnut-scaled brown. I stepped around long mounds, the trunks of great trees fallen years before and riddled into porous skeletons of themselves by fungi and insects. I pushed aside the bare and brittle limbs of spindly dead trees that had lost the battle for light. I crossed a hidden glade that might have been the birthplace of Mama's recent fawns and stepped onto an animal trail which winds through the deciduous thickets, a trail probably as old as the forest and used by many, many four-footed travelers through the years.

The majority of the brushy trees around me were too tall for the deer to be able to reach their leaves, and their smaller shoots had been so eaten during the summer just past that mostly bare, broken stems only remained. Some of these would again put up shoots from their roots; others were dead, among them mountain ash saplings which had been flourishing five years earlier. I looked closely at the twig ends. Deer have a horny pad instead of upper front teeth, so they twist off their browse and leave ragged stem ends. Twigs taken by snowshoe hares look as though they were pruned by a sharp knife. A few of the twig ends were ragged and freshly broken, so I knew that deer came here out of our sight, perhaps Mama and her twins, but most of the twigs were sharp-cut by hares. Even though I had seen hares moving on, they, or perhaps other hares still resident near us, had eaten much of the deer's winter browse.

Under a little washed-out overhang on the hillside, I saw the mound of earth that marks a groundhog's burrow. Gregory might find a mate in the spring. Although ground-hogs were scarce when we moved here, our recent summer visitors had told us of seeing them along the road from town. Their numbers had increased, as had those of the chipmunks and hares in our small domain.

The groundhogs gobbled large quantities of greenery that was especially liked by the hares, and interfered with the production of dandelion seeds, which were a chipmunk stable. The hares, short of greens, ate more of the deer browse. The chipmunks ate more of the wild berries the groundhogs were so fond of. This led the groundhogs to eat more greens and, in turn, the hares to take still more deer food. Meadow mice were also present in such numbers that I saw one or two scooting across the path by the house every day. They were eating more than their normal portion of seeds, leaving fewer to sprout and supply green food for the others next spring. The small herbivores were well on the way to increasing beyond their wild food supply.

I caught movement and looked up to see a barred owl float away like a brown-and-white-striped shadow. At least one predator was still in our woods. I had not seen or heard a wolf, fisher, lynx, bobcat, or mink, and had seen only one fox, in a year. Even weasels were not too plentiful. Bounty hunters and trappers had been very busy, too busy for the good of the forest. Without wolves to control the deer, without lynxes to keep the hares in balance, without foxes to catch the meadow mice, without the thinning of the numbers of the herbivores by all the predators, starvation waited for the deer in some long winter of deep snow yet to come.

I stopped and looked up through the mass of reddish stems and reddening maple leaves, past the white branches and fluttering pale-green leaves of the aspens, to the autumn-blue sky. I was conscious of the absence of the songs of the summer birds, who had quietly moved on. Soon we would have a yard full of migrating juncos and sparrows. I heard no cars or outboards or human voices. The summer guests had gone, too, leaving behind the silence of the woods, which is rarely soundless. There were faint rustles from the leaves, a whir of wings in sudden flight, then a heavy crash in the brush ahead of me. I jumped and my foot slipped. I looked at the path. There was a muddy patch, moistened from underground, and in its center was a huge bear track, just made and slowly filling with water. The bear was preceding me by only a short distance. Keeping a sharp watch, I backed up. I would enjoy seeing the maker of such a track, but not in this enclosed and isolated place.

I came to a break in the thick brush, where the deer had turned aside to come into our yard the previous winter. I stepped onto what remained of their trail, only an indentation in the duff, and hurried away from the bear on the hill.

I emerged from the woods just above the oval pool filled by the small spring that trickles persistently from the side of the bank. The ferns that surrounded the pool moved and, looking away from the place where the bear might be, I saw Mama and her fawns drinking, but before I could more than glimpse their red coats and white uplifted tails they streaked away.

I was surprised that Mama had been so alarmed at seeing me. Then I caught an acrid scent, which must have stung the deer's sensitive noses. Slowly I turned my head to look over my shoulder.

The bear, walking behind me, had come out of the brush to stand under the lofty trees, massive head lifted, nostrils testing the air, a black basalt statue as timeless as the forest itself.

As it moved away and its harsh odor faded, I thought of my early ancestors. No doubt their noses, never offended by the pungent by-products of today's mechanized way of life, would have caught many interesting scents in this air which to me now smelled only of earth and resin and dying leaves. I went back to the cabin with its lamps and its stoves, its clock and typewriter and books, the markers of the generations of civilization behind me. And I knew, feeling a little sad, that by those generations I was forever set apart, an alien in this wild and ancient land.

Mid-October to
December 31

By the middle of October we felt that we could leave
the suet cages hanging outside overnight without danger
of their being stolen by some enterprising bear. It was a
pleasure to no longer be wakened at dawn by woodpeckers
whacking on the logs to remind us to bring out their breakfast, and a relief not to start the day in a kitchen that reeked
every morning with the flat, oily smell of stale suet. In the
rush of fall chores, it was helpful to be rid of even the
small job of taking down and rehanging the feeders.

The oil truck pumped six hundred gallons into our
storage tanks and the last freight delivery brought the
winter groceries. I cleaned shelves and cupboards, then
stuffed them to the last cubic inch with cans and boxes,
hoping that I would remember what was where. Ade went
from window to window, polishing the panes, sealing the
frames with masking tape, and taping on the insulating
plastic sheets. I dug up my dahlia bulbs and tucked them
away under the sofa in a pan of dirt and Ade stored the

feed in garbage cans big enough to hold a hundred pounds each; they were tightly covered against raids by squirrels and mice.

When the warm bronze-and-blue Indian summer came, the fall work was behind us. We slid the boat into the rippling indigo of the lake and, not wanting to break the quiet of the day with the outboard, rowed idly along the shore. We stored in our minds, against the winter soon to come, the red and brown of lichens splotched against gray granite, the blue flash of a late-staying kingfisher, the soft sound of water laving the rocks, the rich commingled scents of the dying summer. As we drifted, the boat began to rise and fall on little swells, the air grew cool on our faces, and distant whitecaps sprang up before a northwest breeze.

We were back at our skid before the rising waves reached us, and as Ade hauled the boat up, he said: "I'll fix her up for winter in the morning. That breeze says we'll light the stove any day now."

I nodded lazily as we walked toward the cabin. "I'm hungry. Wouldn't it be nice to just call somewhere and have them send in egg rolls or ravioli or gefilte fish?"

Ade caught my arms and stopped me. "It would, but you can't have that and our kind of entertainment. Look."

In one of the abandoned garden plots a mass of jewel-weed had grown from scattered seeds. The orange-and-brown flowers were gone, but the four-foot-high plants still held many red-and-green touch-me-not seedpods. A fawn was standing at the edge of the patch of pale green, nosing forward, then arching head and neck back as its touch popped the pods and the seeds peppered its face. It was a comical-looking youngster, having an extra-thick coat and a face so fuzzy that from some angles it looked a little like a buffalo calf.

"I'm surprised it can feel the seeds through all that fur," Ade whispered. "I think it's playing."

And so it seemed. Over and over it pushed into the weeds, ducking back as though trying to move faster than the flying seeds. A pair of black-edged ears appeared beyond the tall plants, a slim beautiful face parted them, and a second fawn walked through the greenery to join the first.

"Mama's twins," Ade breathed into my ear. "She's up on the bank, just out of your sight. Boys or girls, d'you think?"

I looked at the fawns, now munching jewelweed.

"Well—bucks are often bigger, and the pretty one's taller than the other. But their heads are smooth—if they have hair tufts they're too small to see. I say they're both girls. Pretty and Fuzzy—good enough for names?"

"They name themselves," he said. "Fuzzy'll do for either sex, and if you're wrong about Pretty we'll change it to Handsome. They seem fidgety, don't they?"

I watched them stomp, shake their ears, switch their tails.

"Mosquitoes," I said, scratching. "The warm day's brought them out from the dampness under the weeds. Maybe this breeze'll blow them away."

Then Fuzzy had an idea. She moved to the spring and sat down in it, so that the water cooled the bites on her sensitive underparts and dead fern fronds and still-leafy

raspberry canes, swaying in the rising wind, acted as ef-
ficient insect chasers.

I laughed. Fuzzy jumped up and the two fawns, their
eyes wide with wonder and alarm, stared at us before bolting onto the bank and away into the woods with their
mother.

After heavy frosts withered the last leaves, Mama and
her twins came every afternoon for a ration of grain. Their
special spot on the bank was sheltered on one side by a
huge granite boulder and around the back and the other
side by the forest. They had a clear view of the cabin while
they lay quietly resting and chewing.

Mama was unchanged, the same little swaybacked, alert
doe, who was always testing the surroundings with eyes,
ears, nose, and hoofs. Ade commented that her knees were
knobbier than those of many deer and asked, "D'you suppose they got that way from all the stomping?"

Pretty was just that—long-legged and lithe, pearl gray
of coat, graceful of body, and serene of face. Fuzzy was
short and chunky and had a small tumor on the inside of
her left hind leg, which did not seem to bother her, however.

Aside from this, we noticed no sign of disease in the
deer we have known personally. I thought that Peter's poor
condition when we first saw him might be partially due to
something of the kind, but he recovered from his malnutrition so quickly and completely as to make disease unlikely.
However, deer, like people, may have numerous things
wrong with them and show no outward sign, and,
according to some researchers, like humans, they also

seem to be more prone to infection when they are over-crowded.

More than forty internal and external parasites infect whitetails in North America, and several of these affect the welfare of Minnesota deer. Among them are liver flukes, tapeworm cysts, throat bots—which are the larvae of the deer nose fly—and ticks and lice found on the skin and hair. I often see deer licking deep into their fur, maybe to ease the irritation caused by these biting creatures. They do not groom the fur afterward but let it return gradually to its former smoothness. In winter they may so lick their heavy coats that they look as ruffled and bunchy as when they are starting to shed in the spring.

Abscesses, cataracts of the eyes, hernias, and cancerous tumors have been found in deer and are not transmitted to other wild animals or cattle, but certain of their parasitic and infectious diseases may infect other animals. Recently a small, threadlike parasitic roundworm has been found in the tissues surrounding the brain of Minnesota deer. It appears to be common, but apparently does the deer little harm. In 1964 Dr. Keith Loken and Dr. John Schlotthauer of the University of Minnesota College of Veterinary Medicine found these same worms in the heads of moose who were suffering from disorders of the nervous system that have been studied in Minnesota by various workers for more than thirty-five years. This parasite can kill moose and may be a significant control of moose herds. Deer serve as a reservoir host for the parasite and it is reported that the worm is found in moose only when deer are also present. It thus seems unlikely that areas which support many deer may also have a large moose population, like that of northeastern Minnesota in earlier years, before lumbering opened the forest and the whitetails moved into the area from more southerly browsing grounds.

One day I heard a rasping sound from west of the cabin and looked out to see a buck polishing his antlers on the trunk of a little willow tree. His antlers were very fine, with ten long, high points, almost as tall as Peter's of the previous year. Then the buck turned, and there was the notched ear and the slightly closed eye. It *was* Peter. I wondered if the decrease in the size of his antlers meant that he was past the peak of his maturity, and I was puzzled by his coming here so much earlier than usual until I saw him go to the bank and sniff with interest at the spot where Mama had been lying the day before. She was probably approaching her short mating period and Peter with a gleam in his eye had followed her scent.

There was nothing of the gentle buck I knew in his behavior now. He stomped back and forth on the bank, snorting and whacking his antlers against tree trunks. He reared and whirled on his hind legs to strike down at the earth with his forefeet, lowering his head and swaying as though practicing for a fight. Then he rubbed the scent glands inside his hind legs together and walked in widening circles through the brush, as if marking this place as his own, or perhaps making sure that Mama would know he was in the vicinity, should he be absent when she returned.

An hour later Ade, who had been putting braces under the summer-house porch roof as a precaution against collapse from heavy snow, came in, saying, "Guess who I saw in the woods?"

Before I could answer, there was a bump at the door. Standing at the step, antlered head bobbing, pink tongue out, forefoot tapping lightly, was Peter, no longer a warrior ready to fight all comers for his lady, but simply a large and hungry fellow who knew where and how to ask for a hand-out.

After he ate his grain he looked expectantly through the door panel. Sighing, I ground the few carrots I had planned to use for our supper and Ade presented them to Peter.

All afternoon he stayed in the yard, wandering around, occasionally sampling a twig. As evening approached he stepped into the open, head up, ears turned toward the forest. Pretty and Fuzzy pranced down the path, stopped abruptly when they saw Peter, and fled into the woods, perhaps instinctively avoiding this big male of their kind. Mama came slowly to the edge of the bank, then down into the yard, never taking her eyes from Peter, and the two stood motionless, looking at each other. Peter moved toward her and they faced each other, tilting their heads and holding their ears forward. After a minute or two, Mama turned and walked away from him. He followed a little behind her and some fifteen feet to the side. With many starts and stops they moved around the clearing, Peter always looking at Mama, Mama holding her head high and staring off into some place known only to herself.

The twins had returned and were peeking from behind the big boulder on the bank, but neither doe nor buck gave any sign that they knew the fawns were there. Then a car horn sounded on the road. Peter was between Mama and

the possible danger with one leap, standing with his head lowered in fighting position until the car had passed, while Mama waited, not following the car's passing with her ears as she usually did, but completely relaxed as though leaving everything to Peter. When the car had gone, Mama moved quietly to the fawns on the bank. Peter stayed where he was, watching her. Mama led the twins through a stand of infant balsam trees to a secluded place at the foot of a great white pine. Without looking back, she turned away from them and headed into the forest with Peter walking close behind.

While Mama was gone, Pretty and Fuzzy stayed near the cabin, browsing within our sight most of the time, coming each evening for some grain, chewing their cuds and lying down to rest in the spot under the pine where Mama had left them. They seemed to feel quite safe here, but while Pretty showed the expected degree of caution in approaching us Fuzzy seemed to lack this protective instinct. If Ade went out with grain while they were nosing for it under Peter's tree, Pretty trotted off but Fuzzy let him approach almost within touching distance. Pretty avoided strange foods while Fuzzy sampled the willow-bark shreds left by Peter's antler-polishing and found that she had a taste for the tips of little balsam trees. On the other hand, Pretty was undisturbed by sounds from the cabin, but Fuzzy lost her self-possession when I turned on the radio. She stiffened, turned her head and ears in a vain attempt to locate the first music she had ever heard, and, uncertain whether to run or not, compromised by hunching down behind a balsam tree so small that it came only to her shoulder.

On the fourth morning after Mama left with Peter, she rejoined her daughters. The fawns showed no excitement at her return and the three fell into their former routine of browsing, then coming for grain and a rest each afternoon.

Two weeks later a strange buck wandered into the yard, a slim, handsome young fellow with six-point antlers and an infinite capacity for sniffing along trails. Mama kept herself and her fawns well out of his way, bringing them at a fast trot to snatch a few mouthfuls of grain before leaping away again. This went on for two days. Then the buck headed away along the road and we waited for Mama to settle into her old routine.

Long after midnight I heard a stomp and, picking up two cans, one of corn and the other of scratch feed, I stepped out to give the little family group a welcoming banquet. I put half the feed under Peter's tree and decided to take the rest of it over by the big pine, just in case Mama was still a little timid about coming into the open while the young buck's scent was still strong. I did not take a flashlight because I could not carry it along with the two cans. I was picking my way slowly by starlight through the little balsams when there was a snort directly in front of me and I was face to face with the strange buck, who was standing behind the balsams and had probably been watching me out of curiosity.

I am somewhat confused as to what followed. I did not throw the feed at the buck, but think I tossed both cans into the air. He reared, looking as large as a bull moose to me, then pounded away into the woods. I dashed for the cabin, having no trouble at all in finding my way along in the dark this time. I stopped near the door to get my breath and to shake off the grain, which was falling from my hair and sliding down my neck. I even had some in my mouth and was chewing on it.

Then I heard other pounding hoofs and ducked to stand against a tree trunk as Peter thundered past and almost over me, hard on the trail of the intruder. I was just starting away from the tree when Mama came leaping from the direction the two bucks had taken, with the two fawns after her.

It was clouding over and turning ink-dark. I felt besieged by deer and was ready to yell for light when Ade flung open the cabin door and swept the lantern beam across the yard to me.

"What's going on now?" he asked, as we heard a bleating bellow and a crash somewhere to the west.

I ducked gratefully through the light to the doorway and we stood listening to sounds of what was surely a buck fight.

"Peter has caught up with the stranger," I said, giving a sketchy account of the recent happenings.

The uproar did not last long and soon we heard hoofs pounding away again.

"I hope Peter won," I said.

"Of course he did. He outweighs that young fellow by a hundred pounds and with those antlers--don't be silly. It didn't last long enough for the youngster to wear him down. And they haven't locked antlers or anything deadly like that or we wouldn't have heard the loser running away." He paused. "And while I'm thinking about it, you might practice what you preach and not blunder out into the dark in the rutting season. If you must, wake me up and let me cover you with light."

Justly and properly subdued, I went in and combed the grain out of my hair.

Early in November I saw two bucks browsing companionably together in the maple on the hill. I thought this strange for the time of year until they walked into the yard and began to lick up the grain we had scattered for the birds. Pig and Brother, a year and a half old, had come back to us.

They were tall and sleek and still unmistakably individual. Pig had his calculating look and six-point antlers; Brother, his gentle expression, his little mane, and a seven-point rack, with the left antler beam, apparently injured in its formative stages, turned forward over his nose so that he looked like a caribou.

Pig, as might be expected from his childhood brashness, snorted and huffed and grunted, and seemed to think it great sport to chase Pretty and Fuzzy away from the grain. Mama, not at all retiring around her big sons, was having none of this. She watched the fawns retreat, then confronted Pig. He looked up as though to keep her away from the grain, but, ignoring his antlers, she butted his nose. He meekly stepped aside, and after she and the fawns had eaten enough, she went over to him, stretched up to reach his ear, and began to lick behind it vigorously, as she had done when he only reached her shoulder. Truly we had named Mama well.

Pig nosed at the glassed-in flowerbox as he had done before when he wanted grain—and got immediate service.

He was not a patient deer and Ade had no desire to reglaze windows, especially in cold weather. Brother was still his amiable self and I took food to him as confidently as I would to Peter.

One day when the first snowfall was cutting down visibility I did this without first looking around. I had just dumped the corn when Ade yelled from the doorway, "Watch yourself!" Pig, head down and mischief-bent, rushed from behind a tree and I fled to the only available shelter, our biffy. The man who built this rudimentary convenience did not bother to chink it and snow filtered in with every storm, but the openings between the logs gave me an excellent view of Pig, looking pleased with himself, and of Ade, whooping in the kitchen window.

When newspapers on the outside begin to carry notices of our snows and falling temperatures, I receive letters asking *How do you manage to get through your long winters?* I do not believe my answers ever make it clear that, with animal watching, typing, sketching, repair jobs, cooking, and chores, we have little spare time—usually none at all. When we do have, the problem is not how to kill it but what to select from the many things we want to do. Now and then Ade manages to get some project started and, a little now, a little then, brings it to a happy conclusion. The wind-up record player was one of the most successful.

We brought our records with us from Chicago but, not having electricity here, did not move the player. So, when Ade found a spring motor in an ancient and battered Victrola left by the former owners of the log cabin, he rejuvenated a wooden box with a hinged lid, bought pick-ups and diamond needles, assembled the lot with jacks where we could plug in headphones of the type used by radio operators—and we had our music again. The phones had special usefulness because with them I might listen privately to my foreign-language records, whose sounds are among the world's most annoying to someone not interested.

The little player was ready shortly after my flight from Pig, but we were so busy during the next weeks that we had no opportunity to enjoy it. Then Peter came back to lead his small herd. Even Pig was subdued by his size and authoritative manner, and we watched entranced while Peter relaxed under his tree and Mama kept her eye on her big yearling sons and her small daughters.

With the deer and less interesting things to occupy us, we did not slack up for Thanksgiving and Christmas, and it was not until the end of the year that we took our holiday. I stirred up an elaborate buffet-picnic food supply and we settled to relax with our records.

"You know," Ade said, winding the player and handing me my headphones, "all the people we know—they'd never understand why we aren't bored or lonely up here."

I nodded, listening to the zero-cold snow creaking under the deer's hoofs, the snap of a cabin log as the night temperature fell, and the hoot of a hunting owl.

"What'll we play first?" I asked.

"Why—'Auld Lang Syne.' What else?"

January 3
to Mid-April

On the third day of the New Year whose coming we had celebrated with our records a storm arrived without warning and with only the faintest whispers, a steady vertical dropping of fine crystals, soft white by day and glittering gold by night as they passed through the lamplight from the windows. After thirty hours of this dim and hidden world the sky cleared and the sun shone on a strange landscape. The laden branches drooped, and slender trees arched over an expanse of white unbroken by anything except the tree boles. Bushes, little evergreens, the woodpile, and paths were covered. From the cabin, smooth white stretched to the shore, over its buried rocks, and onto the frozen lake. The only sound was the muffled grinding of the ice, not yet thick enough to bear the great weight of snow without cracking.

Our door swings inward, and when I opened it soft snow slid into the kitchen. Ade, who intended to use his

snowshoes to tramp down our paths, put them back on
their hooks on the wall.

"I'll have to shovel," he said. "The shoes would sink
into that stuff and pick up ten pounds on the toes at every
step."

I swept the melting snow out of the kitchen as soon as
he made an open space outside the door, and threw grain
there for the birds and squirrels, who had appeared on cue
when the door opened. He was shoveling around Bedelia's
little house when the deer came floundering out of the
maple, Peter in the lead, his chest acting as a plow. Mama,
apparently very hungry, turned aside to pass him. She
sank in almost to her shoulders and made her way by
laborious, straining lunges.

Once the deer were near the cabin, their hoofs soon
trampled and packed the snow so that they could move
about easily. They stayed in the yard for the next week,
the adults making short trips into the woods, but always
leaving one behind to keep an eye on little Pretty and
Fuzzy. If either of them started toward the woods, the
"baby-sitter" administered disciplinary whacks on the
rump. At first I thought this was some matter of training.
Then I wondered if wolves, not in the vicinity for a year,
might be near again.

Then I decided to go into the woods myself. I plowed
my way through snow above my knees to the top of the
bank and was following its edge when I misjudged my
direction. A step took me into neck-deep snow in the
drainage ditch. There is only one way to get out of deep
snow—to dig your way ahead, standing up while you do it.
You cannot help yourself by pushing down with your
hands because they only go on down and you bury yourself

more deeply. Attempts to climb up dislodge small avalanches that pack in around you. As I pushed and made swimming motions to clear my way toward the cabin, I saw Mama with the two fawns standing on one of the deer trails. No wonder the fawns were guarded. I remembered the fawn's leg Jacques had showed me two years before. That young deer, deep in snow as I was, had struggled to exhaustion, from which death is not far off in energy-sapping cold. Perhaps an adult deer might trample a path through which a trapped fawn could escape from snow, much as Ade was shoveling toward me, but I have never seen any indication of deer's thinking in this way.

By the time I had changed clothes and warmed up it was dark. The next morning I went exploring again, this time prudently following the deer trails. They had walked over and over the same routes, churning and packing the snow into narrow ways that were reasonably easy traveling for me. Where the snow was deepest, the sides of the trails were brushed back by their bodies, and this piled-up snow heightened the tunnel-like effect produced by the relative narrowness of the trails and the overhanging, snow-heavy brush.

The main deer trail coincided with the ancient animal trail across the hill. I passed the place where I had seen the bear track the previous fall and turned into one of the many interlocking side trails the deer had made. They crossed and curved and turned back on themselves, patterned with the dainty marks of hoofs. I remembered how Peter's trails during his first winter with us were so many and so scattered that even Jacques, with all his woods lore, thought we had more than one deer coming regularly to the yard.

I was getting chilly, so I turned into another trail that I thought would bring me out under the big trees between our cabins. A few minutes later I climbed over a hummock and found myself at the edge of the road. I had not been more than three hundred feet from either cabin during my walk and, with the sky overcast and no sun to guide me, had lost my way as completely as though I were in strange country. The plow had not yet come through and the snow sloped from the high south bank across the road to my feet. I was tired enough not to want to struggle through such a drift so I turned back into the maze of deer trails. This time I would keep going down hill. I couldn't miss my way if I did.

Suddenly a white tail flashed ahead of me and I saw Mama bolting from the sound of my approach. I spoke softly and she stopped, turned, and watched me. Pretty was just behind her in this secret world of the white tunnels, her fine tail spread to look like a leaf-shaped, black-tipped fan outlined by white fringe. When Mama relaxed, so did Pretty, and the hairs realigned themselves into the tail's ordinary, narrower shape.

Then Mama switched her tail and walked away, and Pretty switched her tail and followed. This tail-switching before walking from a standing position is so regular an action that Ade says he has a feeling that it unlocks their hind legs so that they can move!

I got back to the yard without further confusion, but only by keeping to the fresh tracks of the two deer.

All three bucks had lost their antlers in December. Peter held his position by size and age, I think, with Mama second-in-command. Brother was quiet and Pig inordinately curious. He had a disconcerting way of hiding beside the cabin and suddenly poking his head around a corner, ears spread wide and eyes popping, as though to make sure he did not miss anything.

Peter kept much to himself, standing aside and watching the others, while Mama kept order with her stomping forefeet. When she wanted a place at the grain she bore down on Pig and Brother, who ran out of her way with heads lowered and tails down. I noticed that Mama also ran with her tail down except when she headed away and the growing young does followed her, as though her uplifted white flag were a guide for them.

I wondered whether this flag was as much of an alarm signal as I had heard, until a character in a twin-engined Cessna buzzed our cabin. The deer were used to the passing of an occasional small plane, its occupants perhaps making a forestry survey, but the roar of the swooping Cessna set them quivering and jerking, trying to locate the noise. As the plane came to the bottom of its foolhardy dive, barely missing the tops of our tallest trees, the deer leaped away in six different directions, all of them with their tails up.

That night the air warmed and a light rain fell, which by morning had turned into freezing drizzle. Ade and I followed its progress anxiously. All life in the wilderness, including ours, is ruled by the weather, and a layer of ice, which in a city would mean only an overworked bureau of sanitation and late arrivals at work, may bring disaster to the woods.

The leaves of the cedars were slowly coated and webbed as though encased in clear plastic, and the tops of the great trees began to sag under the weight of ice. Now and then there was a snap and a tinkling crash as a small branch gave way. It was with great relief that we felt a freezing wind come out of the North. Before the ice accumulated to a point beyond the bearing of the trees, the drizzle turned into light snow. But when the sky cleared, the fallen seeds were frozen into an inch-thick crust, the tree-borne cones and buds were armored with ice, and the insect eggs in the tree bark were shut away as though behind glass.

Ade cut down a cluster of cedar cones, which we thawed and dried, then shook for seeds. Most of them had already fallen and would not be available to the birds until the crust melted. Hoping to help birds that did not eat our usual grains, we added cornmeal, rice, crumbs, and MPF. A female evening grosbeak who had been picking up cedar seeds in the yard every day went elsewhere to look for food, but the jays, chickadees, nuthatches, and woodpeckers came in flocks. The yard boiled with life. I have never seen so many of these birds here at any other time, and I think that strangers, flying around looking for food, saw our regular visitors and joined them.

Ade brought the suet cages in to thaw out. Hairy and downy woodpeckers squealed their annoyance, then by experiment found that they could eat oatmeal, picking it up with their sticky tongues and scooping it with the side of their beaks. Some forty pine siskins fluttered down to eat MPF. We rarely see them so close as they usually cluster to feed in a treetop, then burst out of it and fly in a scattered flock to another, making their characteristic buzzing, zinging sound. Three of them discovered a cache of cedar seeds caught between the permanent screen and the sill outside the window by my typewriter. They hopped along, tiny, heavily streaked birds with their bright yellow patches on wing and tail, picking up the seeds less than two feet from me, keeping as close an eye on me as I did on them.

By mid-afternoon, although the air temperature was only twenty, the ice began to melt in the strong sunlight. Next morning the rough gray-white snow crust, glittering with ice particles fallen from the trees, was separated into wavering bands by thin ribbons of greenish ice. It looked like watered silk trimmed with crystal beads. The siskins returned to feed in their treetops and we knew that although the snow was still crusted, the danger of a bird catastrophe was over.

We wondered about the deer, whose squirrel-cut cedar leaves were frozen into the crust. They came in the afternoon, hesitating, uneasy, listening to the strange tinkling and shushing sounds of the ice still shattering in the breeze, watching the sky as though to make sure that whatever had come with such a loud noise was no longer here.

As Peter was leading them carefully down their smoothest trail into the yard, something alarmed them and they leaped away, their hoofs crashing through the crust, their legs plunging past the sharp edges of the broken ice. When they returned later we saw abrasions on their legs and spots rubbed bare. Fuzzy, limping from a bad gash on the upper part of one leg, slipped and slid on the ice hummocks and had great difficulty in keeping on her feet.

I thought most unkindly of the supercilious pilot who had thought to startle some backwoodsmen and had succeeded only in frightening these harmless animals away from our sheltered place. Had they stayed and moved back and forth on their trails, they would have broken the ice as it formed and had little difficulty. Ade looked at the sky and said: "It wouldn't hurt my feelings any if that fool had his wings ice up and made a forced landing. Then he could share the fun of being afraid and going hungry and trying to drag himself through this mess!"

I was trying unsuccessfully to make myself say something about the thought being uncharitable, when Mama blew and the deer hurried away over the trail they had just broken. A long-legged, short-tailed animal crossed the path and disappeared into the woods before I could say "Bobcat!"

Ade was looking a little ahead of where it disappeared and said, almost at the same moment, "Lynx!"

This went on for most of the evening. I was sure the cat had the bobcat's short ear tufts and Ade was equally sure it had the lynx's long ones. I insisted that it was strongly marked; he said that it was shaded gray. It had been too far away for us to see whether the tail tip was black on top only for a bobcat or black all around for a lynx. We gave up the futile argument after we took a lantern to look for tracks and found the crust too hard to show any, but not strong enough to bear our weight.

Ade shook me awake at dawn.

"Come quick. The lynx is in front of the kitchen window."

The night before I had set out a roasting pan so that birds might pick the bits of meat and grease. The lynx was crouched with forepaws on the edge of the pan and was licking it, not daintily as a cat usually does but with such strength that the pan moved ahead and the cat followed in little jumps. The lynx is wary and is usually nocturnal. This one had been driven into the dangerous daylight, and the even more dangerous presence of man, by hunger.

He attacked the pan, trying with teeth too long for the task to get a few morsels of food from it. His haunches were almost skin and bones, and not even the long hairs of his coat could hide his emaciated ribs. At last he moved aside, slowly, with stiff hind legs and hanging head, and sat to lick his paws. The sun broke through clouds and, as the warmth touched him, he lay down wearily in front of the window and dozed.

His fur was thick and gray, like ruffled, deep-piled plush, with faint spotting on his lower sides and legs and a darker shading down his spine. He had a reddish snub nose, eyes like disks from a harvest moon, faint black face stripings, and luxuriant whiskers. His black ear tufts were more than an inch and a half long. The whiteness of his thick ear-to-ear ruff was broken by two black splotches, one on each side of his jaw, and its hairs met in a point below his mouth, like a white Vandyke beard.

Suddenly he turned his head and we saw that the backs of his ears were black around the outside and white in the center.

"There's my bobcat," I murmured to Ade, as a striped cat stepped from behind a tree.

We expected a fight, but the bobcat merely waited while the lynx rose and returned to again attack the pan. When at last he pushed back, stretched his long hind legs, and walked away, we saw his oversized feet and stubby tail, tipped with black as though dipped in ink. By comparison with Bedelia's fence, we estimated that he was nineteen inches tall at the rump and thirty-eight inches long, without his four-inch tail. He was about one fifth larger than the bobcat and, when properly fattened up, should weigh about forty pounds. As he dragged himself away,

Ade said: "Poor, hungry Big Cat!" and our visiting lynx was named.

The bobcat was busy with the pan now. This animal was thin, but showed its still-good physical condition by supple, graceful movements and sleek, glossy fur. It had a typical tiger-cat face, with glowing yellow eyes marked around with white and a reddish snub nose like the lynx's, but more strongly outlined with black. Its black-and-white-striped ruff spread like bushy whiskers from the sides of its face and curled forward in two little points under its receding chin. Its forehead and the top of its head were reddish and lightly striped with black. Its upstanding, slightly pointed ears bore short black hair tufts and were marked on the back like its companion's. Its legs, shading from white to pearl gray, were lavishly cross-striped with black and its rusty coat was richly spotted and marked. Its five-inch tail, constantly curling and twisting, was splotched with black on top but white underneath.

A few minutes later it left the pan, stretched and stared wide-eyed up the hill, and walked away, springing on its dainty paws.

"It moves like a tiger," I said, and Tiger the bobcat became.

"They aren't enemies," Ade said. "Do you think they're traveling together? Maybe to help each other find food?"

"I never heard of such a thing, but it looks like it. We'll know if they hang around awhile."

Fortunately we had just received a large supply of suet and scrap meat from our butcher. We put out equal portions, one under Peter's tree and the other ten feet away. The two cats came from the brush as soon as we were back in the cabin, Tiger leading the way down a deer trail. They ate separately and without any clash, and when the food was gone went as they had come, except that they disappeared together under our storage building. That they were companions we did not doubt now. Many old-timers believe that gray bobcats are produced by cross-matings of bobcat and lynx. Although we never discovered Tiger's sex, Ade and I do not ignore the possibility that our feline traveling companions might have been a mated pair. They roamed, moused, and hunted hares separately, and Big Cat had a private retreat under a tarpaulin that protected the woodpile, but almost every night during the two months they made our yard their headquarters we could see the two pairs of eyes glowing green in a flashlight beam, watching from under the storage building until we brought out food for them.

On the evening of the cats' arrival, Ade put grain under the tree as usual, but the deer would not come in. Mama started blowing on the bank and Peter, Pig, and Brother joined in. Even Pretty and Fuzzy made small sniffing sounds. So Ade took grain to the open space in the forest where Mama had once brought Snowboots to eat cedar. This was a hundred feet or so from the cats' temporary den, and the deer accepted the arrangement at once, posting a guard to keep watch in the direction of possible danger.

Later we heard the deer guard blowing and looked out to see Big Cat approaching the suet in the yard and Tiger sitting outside the storage building. The adult deer changed guard at short intervals and all fed quickly. Once Pretty stepped up to take her turn, but Peter nudged her back to the grain. Apparently keeping watch against two meat-eaters of this size was a job for experienced deer only.

The cats did not approach the deer, but the deer, as if to test the cats' reaction, decided to use one of their trails which lay about fifteen feet in front of the storage building. Peter and Mama led the way, walking slowly and tensely, heads low and turned toward the building. When nothing happened, they hurried past with quick, nervous little steps, then bounded ahead and stood watching while the two fawns followed and Pig and Brother, moving as Peter and Mama had, seemed to be protecting their rear. They did this every afternoon and we knew when the cats were absent because Peter and Mama relaxed their vigilance when they came near the building, either hearing nothing or smelling no fresh scent. On one occasion near the end of the cats' visit, Big Cat, no longer weak and thin, was approaching the building in the open when the deer family came into view. He hastily retreated, possibly having no desire to chance being slashed and trampled by all those sharp hoofs.

There is no question but that bobcats and lynxes can, and occasionally do, kill deer, probably by dropping from a branch or ledge when a deer passes the right place at the right time and speed. However, a cat, clinging to the back of a terrified deer bounding through thick woods, would be in great danger of being brained against a tree. Any deer large enough to run could outdistance one of these cats on the ground. We watched both Tiger and Big Cat look covetously at a hanging suet feeder in the yard, but neither of them attempted to jump *up*, although the cage was less than two feet out of reach of their forepaws when they rose and tried to bring it down. It thus seems doubtful that either would attempt to jump up to the much more uncertain target of a running deer's throat or back. Considering that deer populations expand in the absence of wolves while their browse does not, the herd would probably benefit if wild cats did take some of them.

Early in April, when the south winds began to push the melting snow away from the first patches of bare ground, Peter and Pig and Brother left for their summering place. Then Mama disappeared, leaving Pretty and Fuzzy alone. We had not seen the cats for a week and felt sure that they had gone, else Mama would not separate from her young daughters. As traffic increased, Pretty and Fuzzy went too, and the yard seemed strangely empty with only the bright-colored squirrels and just-emerged chipmunks to represent our neighbors in fur.

Water began to gurgle under the remaining snow and I went to the shore to look across the ice once more before its white snow covering should be swallowed by the run-off from the hills. As I stared into the distance, I wondered how the starving ones, like Peter and Tiger and Big Cat, found Ade and me in the midst of all the wilderness they might wander through. Ice fishermen had seen a bobcat and a lynx cross the ice from Canada in February—Big Cat and Tiger, surely. But where were they now?

The slanting sunlight brought into shadowed relief some marks out from the shore. I waded through slush that was deepening above a crack in the ice and looked at a double line of tracks, melting but still clear—the neat, four-toed marks of a bobcat's feet and the big, snowshoe tracks of a lynx. Tiger and Big Cat, fat and rested and strong, had gone home.

the
fourth
year

THE
LONG
ROAD

Mid-May
to November 17

The green that marks the northward progress of spring
flows around our north-facing slope and comes together
again on the sunwashed Canadian shore across the lake.
From the air, the two shores look much alike at this time.
In the forested portions, new-leaved aspen and birch tops
stretch like rolling meadows between the black-green of
spruce and pine. Waves of shaded green cover the open
spots. From the ground, the sunny shore is clear of snow,
even in the hidden places, and the open green breaks into
masses of bracken, clumps of leafy raspberry canes, and
areas of new grass with white and purple violets in bloom.
But our shaded earth seems a month behind, with snow
and ice still lingering here and there, the fiddleheads of the
ferns just venturing to uncoil, the raspberries only budding, and no flowers except the catkins on the willows and
birches.

In the middle of May, four weeks after the wild cats
left us, I sat on the cabin doorstep watching for something

that had the quality of the season according to the calendar. The sun's gilding and lifting of the morning mist, the soft coolness of the air, the faint hum of insects were of the spring, but also of the summer and the fall. Perversely, I wanted something special, much as I had on the Christmas afternoon when Peter came out of the forest. And, as he had come, so now Pretty stepped from the softly leaved maple.

How can I tell you of such beauty? She tiptoed through the swirls of mist on hoofs of polished jet. The light covered her slimness with a brocade of red-gold and shone rosily through ears like the uplifted petals of some marvelous opening flower. The gentleness of her slender face was heightened by shadings of gray, faintly touched with violet. Her great dark eyes looked from under their peaked eyebrow markings with the shy innocence of a child. Youth and spring had come to me in the form of a yearling doe.

She drifted across the yard to the muddy hollow where we throw the water from the kitchen and began to lick the mud with long sweeps of her pink tongue. When Ade came back with the mail an hour later she was still licking.

We stood watching her, and he said, "If she needs minerals, why doesn't she nibble the compost heap? Mama did last spring. Or chew on that rotted cedar stump the deer are tearing away?"

"I think she wants salt. The salt from my cooking water is in that mud. We've enough deer to need a big block."

"Salt!" he said, whacking his palm against his forehead. "Jacques left a salt block at the top of the path before he cleared out for Canada! I put it in the storage building and never thought of it again."

"Well—" I said. "It's only been a year and a half!"

He moved to and from the building without Pretty's even looking up and set the fifty-pound white block atop a stump near Peter's tree.

A half hour passed before Pretty moved away from the mud lick. There was a faint drift of air across the salt block and when she came in line with it she stopped. She spread her nostrils, raised and lowered her head, turned to face into the air's flow. Step by step, sniffing and testing the air along the ground, she moved thirty feet to find the block of salt. And I know people who are not quite convinced that an animal can smell something which to human nostrils is quite odorless.

The next day Fuzzy joined her sister, and what a contrast! Fuzzy's coat was ruffled, her upper lip overhung her lower one slightly at the sides, and her chinline sagged. Her ears flapped without much purpose and she pottered around the yard, sometimes stumbling over a stone or a fallen branch, then looking at her feet as though she could not understand how they could be so clumsy. She was so little interested in sudden noises and changes in the yard that Ade said she acted as though she took tranquilizers. And she simply loved people. She bumped around the cabin at night until one of us came out to feed her, then stood so near that we had to shoo her out of the way. She ambled up behind two ladies who had come to ask me to autograph a book, and nudged one of them in the ribs. She was too fearless for her own good, but we could not tell her that.

One night I went to get corn from the big storage can near Bedelia's house, and Fuzzy came right along, bent on seeing where I got the feed perhaps. As I came abreast of the coop, a big barred owl took flight from its top—almost touching Fuzzy's ears. Moving faster than I thought she could, she turned and bounded out of sight with her tail up. She was back the next day and treated Ade as usual, but I was definitely *persona non grata*. She backed off from me with her ears laid back and the expression of a bad-tempered mule on her face, and did not forgive me for throwing the owl at her for all of two weeks.

She soon learned that if she stuck her nose forward Ade would let her eat out of the can in his hand. Since she seemed to be always hungry, this must have been very satisfactory, for she could guzzle without having to share with Pretty, who might nose into the same grain pile on the ground.

One afternoon near the first of June Ade was holding out the feed can and Fuzzy was sauntering over to it, when there came a loud blowing and a stomp from the bank. Fuzzy's ears flipped to attention and she turned to face Mama, unexpectedly returned and distributing her reprimands equally between Ade and Fuzzy. They backed away from each other, both keeping an eye on Mama, in case she should come down from the bank to emphasize her warning with her hoofs. Fuzzy strolled away and Ade dumped the grain on the ground and ducked inside.

"That'll teach you," I snickered.

"Maybe I'm adopted," he said.

Mama, who had followed him to the door, blew once more, as though to say she might have expected such foolishness from Fuzzy but that Ade should have had better sense.

We were thrilled at the thought of having the three does with us in summer, but Pretty grew nervous when the voices of hiking vacationers began to come from the road and outboards followed the shoreline, carrying first-time visitors on tours of inspection. She came a few nights for a good measure of salt, then quietly went away. Fuzzy took all human sounds as a matter of course and spent hours standing by the recording rain gauge which Ade tends for the U. S. Weather Bureau. She turned her ears toward it as though listening to the voice of its clockwork, and now and then gave it a companionable lick.

I grew nervous myself as the days passed with almost no rain and the smoke of distant forest fires spread yellow mist across our sky, but Ade very practically said that one good thing about a dry summer was the amount of outside work he could get done.

"The roof, for instance. It's already waited two years. All we need is a drizzle to have water pouring through all over the house."

"And we can't even start to remodel inside with all those leaks," I added.

"First things first. You entertain yourself with visions of the redone interior. I'll take care of the roof."

So in mid-June he was sitting beside the chimney, calculating areas and the number of rolls of roofing we would need, while I stared up from the yard and wondered whether green might not look better than red, or maybe blue—or one of those aluminized colors that had a silvery cast. He had tucked pad and pencil into his pocket, picked up his steel tape, and started to move to another roof section, when he froze in a half-risen position, put a finger to his lips, and made little gestures toward the west. I turned my head very slowly.

Mama stood at the edge of the woods, head thrust forward, forefoot lifted and ready to stomp. I looked up at Ade and was about to speak, but he shook his head slightly and wiggled a finger at a row of interrupted ferns between the path into the forest and the big pine. I gradually turned and saw the tips of two pairs of little ears between the fronds. I held my breath.

Slowly Mama backed away and the ears moved toward her through a clump of balsam saplings. Then she came to a grassy spot where her favorite bluebead lilies grew. She stopped to nip off a plant and her new fawns moved shyly to her on still-wobbly legs.

They were not much taller than the lilies and their white-spotted red coats made them almost a part of the sun-dappled forest carpet. Their eyes were wide and dark and full of wonder. Either of them could have found room and to spare for all four hoofs on the palm of my hand. One of them, with a white star on its forehead, took shelter in the safest place it knew—under Mama's belly. It lost interest in us soon and nudged Mama's udder, but she drew aside and led her twin miracles into seclusion.

I stood looking at the place where they had gone out of sight, remembering how Peter had courted Mama and wondering, if their fawns were bucks, whether they might not grow to be as strong and beautiful as Peter, and have his gentle, generous disposition.

Somewhere nearby, within the last four or five days, Mama had given birth to these incredibly lovely six-pound children. I could picture her, glowing with pride, washing them thoroughly with her tongue, lying quietly while they took their first meal from her; then, as soon as they could stand with reasonable steadiness, leading them away from their place of birth, to which her scent might bring predators. I could see them resting in some hidden place, waiting for her to return from getting her own food and give them their milk.

To protect them from her scent, Mama would stay away from her little ones as much as possible during their first month. Lying motionless, having almost no scent of their own, and blending as they do with leaves and shadows, the defenseless infant fawns are amazingly safe alone. I once was following a forest trail when a straying dachshund crossed in front of me. I stopped to see where it might be going and was startled when a fawn leaped up, only a few feet from me and about a yard from where the dog had passed. The fawn made a sound almost like a bird call and ran to greet its mother, who came crashing through the brush, alarmed by either my scent or that of the dog. Had the fawn been frightened away before she reached it, she might have trailed it by the secretion of the glands in its hoofs.

As nearly as I could figure, Mama's twins were born two hundred thirteen days after she had gone away with Peter the previous fall. This is not too accurate as a length of the gestation period because Mama was away four days with Peter and the fawns might have been a little younger or older than I guessed. Twins are the usual birth, although we have known does whose first matings produced single fawns. Quadruplets and even quints have been reported, but we have not seen even the more common triplets. There was once a runt deer in the yard, whom Jacques thought might have been one of triplets and stunted because it was weaker than its siblings and unable to get a sufficient supply of milk. It might also have been a pygmy from birth or orphaned before it was completely weaned, and undersized from having to subsist on vegetation only before it was old enough. However, I once knew a pair of motherless fawns who grew normally although orphaned when quite small.

Mama's delivery was within the usual fawning time for this area, from mid-May through June, although numbers of fawns arrive earlier in May and somewhat fewer in July. There are even out-of-season matings and births. If born late, fawns may not survive their first winter because they are not yet wearing their winter woollies when the cold comes, or because they are too small and weak to fight through the deep snow to get food. If born early, their baby coats may not be adequate protection through the uncertain transition weather between winter and spring. On the other hand, in September 1965 I saw a doe with a pair of young bucks whose bodily development and antler growth was that of *yearlings* in *June*. From their appearance, they had been born the previous August or September and had survived the onset of winter, to be weaned and get their winter coats around the end of 1964.

Although Mama was exceptional among does we have observed in that she mothered every one of her children, no matter how large they had grown, all does are devoted mothers and never willingly abandon their fawns. Only the capture or death of the mother leaves her little ones alone. Sometimes well-meaning people find a fawn and take it away, thinking it is orphaned. If a young wild creature survives being reared by humans and is then returned to its natural home, it is seriously handicapped by the lack of training that only its own kind can give. It may also be confused and lonely in a place unlike the only home it has known, and may be less healthy than it would have been had it been nourished on its mother's milk. Deer milk, for instance, is three times as rich in fat and protein as cow's milk. If fawns are removed from the place where their mother left them, she can find no trail but will search long and pitifully, calling in faint bleating sounds. It is best not to touch fawns, because this not only shocks and frightens them but also gives them the human scent, which may attract domestic dogs or cats. Mother deer will bathe a youngster who carries the scent of man very thoroughly, starting at its tail and going over it with her tongue to the tip of its ears and nose, until it once again does not smell at all, as is proper for a baby deer.

The summer was quieter than usual, possibly because vacationers were uneasy about coming so far on a one-way road into a forest where crackling dry duff and sometimes the smell of smoke reminded them of the fire danger. For some unknown reason the bears were elsewhere. With these two threats to her fawns out of the way, Mama stayed nearby and occasionally ate the corn Ade left for her at the edge of the forest. She had been very thin when we first saw her with her twins and the concentrated ration helped her regain her lost weight quickly.

One afternoon in August Fuzzy looked up from her everlasting nibbling and began to show more animation than she had since the night of her unfortunate encounter with the owl. Only this time she was all interest—ears twitching, nostrils wide and sniffing, tail moving in quick little jerks. She danced about, then leaped to meet Mama, who was approaching the bank with her fawns.

While Mama and Fuzzy exchanged greetings, the little ones, now slim-legged, sure of step, and about eighteen inches high at the rump, fidgeted this way and that, looking with the liveliest interest at Fuzzy, the cabin, Ade and me in the window. Everything was new and strange, and although they stayed where they were—and Mama kept turning to make sure that they did—they plainly wanted to explore.

The next weeks are still as clear in my mind as yesterday, and I hope they always will be. While Mama and Fuzzy browsed and ate their grain and rested on the edge of the bank, the twins took over our yard. They rolled in the tall grass of the clearing, drank together from the tiny spring, reared on their slim legs to box, rushed up to Fuzzy as she lay resting and pattered their front hoofs on her paunch, then were gone before she could more than lift a hoof to wave them away. They chased each other across the clearing and through the forest, raced on the path, sampled leaves and berries and flowers—two white-dotted, red-gold sprites; quick, dainty, lovely beyond dreams; exuberant and joyful in their quiet, safe world.

Gradually their neat, camouflaging spots disappeared

and they were a smooth red, which blended with the falling leaves of late September as their spotted coats had made them part of the summer scene. Pre-antler tufts of reddish hair became prominent on their foreheads, and we named the slightly smaller one Little Buck and the one with the white blaze above his eyes Starface.

Slowly, as the frosts of October brought down the leaves, the deer's coats began to thicken and take on the gray of winter. Little Buck and Starface, still small but growing heavier and developing sturdy bodies, began to enjoy more adult games. Little Buck often stood in the clearing, head high and ears alert, and stomped over and over, looking toward Mama now and then as though asking whether he was going about this in proper fashion. Starface whirled on his hind legs and struck lightly at the ground, pawed the earth and swept his head from side to side, much as Peter had done when he arrived the year before. Sometimes they squared away, pawing the moss and striking at each other. Then they lowered their heads in fighting position, pressed the tops of their heads together, and shoved back and forth until one or the other rolled over, to be dealt quick, token blows by the winner of the bout. Mama watched all this complacently, as though nothing could please her more than to have her little fellows growing up with the correct competitive instincts.

Occasionally Little Buck fell from grace and decided he was still small enough to nurse. Mama first walked away from his searching mouth. If he followed, she switched her tail vigorously in his face. When this did not discourage him, she whirled and dealt him a smart whack on the head, which set him shaking his ears and withdrawing from his infant food supply.

Starface's weakness was butterflies. He tried his best to catch every one he saw by flicking at it with his tongue. He did not, to my knowledge, ever get one. When a cloud of migrating Monarchs fluttered into the yard, he almost went wild, leaping, jumping, licking frantically at the orange-and-black flowerlike insects. Perhaps their very unusualness added to his excitement. He had seen nothing like them, and neither had we. Perhaps they were blown off course as this was their only appearance here. I hoped that they would settle on one of our bushes, but Starface scattered them with his antics and they drifted on, leaving him to stare foolishly after them.

The days continued to be mild and the light frosts left some hardy greenery for the deer in the wild country to feed on, but Ade and I kept a sharp watch for the rest of the small herd. Pretty arrived near the end of October, taller than the others, more graceful, paler of coat and face. Two weeks later Pig and Brother walked down the path. They were larger and heavier than they had been the year before and both had perfect eight-point antlers. Pig still had that wicked gleam in his eye and Brother still looked gentle as a doe.

In spite of the bucks' size and antlers, Mama remained the boss. She kept order at the grain piles, pushing Pig around when he showed signs of acting as he had when he was the size of Little Buck and Starface. Once he poked her not too gently in the rump with his antlers. She tucked in her rear as she jumped aside and turned to give him a resounding thump on the bridge of his nose. He seemed to pay not the slightest attention to this attempt at discipline, but I noticed that he did not use his antlers against her again.

Little Buck kept out of the way of his big brothers, but Starface developed an acute case of hero-worship for Pig and trailed him around the yard, hopefully reaching out his nose for a friendly lick. Pig responded by chasing Starface round and round, away from the grain and into the woods, never really trying to overtake him, but just being fractious. Starface seemed delighted with all this attention and came back regularly for more.

Most of the time Pig and Brother were not too far apart, sometimes running through the woods like young horses, sometimes standing together licking their fur. Mama and her daughters were not ready for mating and I felt sure that there were no other does in the near distance; else the two bucks would have been roaming.

Shortly after the bucks returned we had one of those stirring late-fall days, when the high wind sings and your blood stirs in answer to its song. Knowing that winter was hanging heavy overhead, I could not stay indoors. I went for a long walk on the road, stopping to watch the brook weave frills and laces over its stones, listening to the last calls of the crows, scenting the smoky richness of autumn, and reveling in the sun on my face. I met a friend driving by and we exchanged pleasant comments on the weather and the last migrating birds.

When I came down the hill to the edge of our clearing, Pretty and Fuzzy were lying side by side on the bank, chewing rhythmically and enjoying the warm, quiet afternoon. Pig and Brother stood in the open; first one, then the other, folded a front leg, dropped to his knees, and lay down in the dry grass for a snooze. Mama and her youngest twins stood near the big bucks. Little Buck nuzzling her neck and Starface squinting away from having his face washed. Bedelia was taking the last dust bath of the season and Ade was standing, her empty feed pan in his hand, watching the deer.

As I slowly came on to become part of this scene of deep peace and content, I thought of the words of an ancient king:

> He maketh me to lie down in green pastures:
> he leadeth me beside the still waters.

November 18 to
December 2

I woke with a start the next morning, wide awake and listening for some unusual sound, but I heard nothing except the chittering of two squirrels, who each wanted sole possession of the woodshed. Ade was still sleeping. I must have dreamed the sound. I glanced idly at the clock and the calendar, looked more intently at the sky losing its grayness in the dawn light, and decided that a walk before breakfast would be perfect.

I made the coffee while I dressed, gulped a cup, and went into the woods between the cabins just as the first rays of the sun touched the treetops, whose pointed shadows now reached toward the northwest. The long summer days had gone with the northeastern rising of the sun and soon, so very soon, the sun beams would be shut off from the cabin all day by the southern hills. My footsteps crunched in the too dry leaves and needles and I was glad that we could soon expect snow to end the fire danger.

But now, even at a little after seven, the air was already warm and still full of the autumn harvest scents.

I followed the animal trail and, in the spot which is always damp from an underground spring, saw big deer tracks. Pig or Brother had walked here not long before me. I idled along the hidden trail, and found myself starting to plan a series of children's stories, based on Pig and Brother, with overtones of Starface and Little Buck. My pair of fawns would be something like the mischievous twin bear cubs, Cuno and Bruno, whose adventures my father had created to amuse me when I was small. I tried to recall some of their comical actions and wondered if I could make little Pig and Brother as much fun to read about and if I should let them grow up. I'd have to think of better names. . . .

The crash of a heavy rifle racketed through the woods, and then another, not a hundred feet from me. The date, which had not registered as I looked at the calendar earlier, flashed behind my eyes and I knew that the deer season was open—and that someone had found the tame deer. I yelled but got no answer. Suddenly I wanted to meet these people who shot within sight of a house in a yard protected, we had thought, by NO HUNTING signs. I hurried along the trail, shouting.

"Listen! There's another one!" came a man's voice.

I turned cold. This man was so excited that he did not hear my shouts and was conscious only of the crackling, breaking branches, which meant "deer" to him. Someone might shoot at the sound. And I was on a deer trail, in thick shrubbery and heavy shadow, dressed in navy blue from head to foot. With the thought, I dropped flat behind a low ridge of rock and earth and saw that I was near a side trail, made by the deer as they came into the yard from the road. Its brush was broken away and its leaves trampled to dusty powder, so that I could slither along almost noiselessly—quietly enough that the hunters would not hear me, anyway. I heard a scuffling sound and knew that they were dragging the dead deer to the road.

If I hurried I could confront them in the open. They wouldn't hear me now. They were too occupied with moving the carcass. Carcass. An odd way to think of one of those deer who had rested so peacefully by the log cabin only a few hours before. I stood up and ran, but the windings of the little trail made me too slow. When I jumped onto the road, I glimpsed a car with an out-of-state license disappearing around a curve.

I was shaking and felt sick, so I sat down on a rock and closed my eyes. As though my eyelids were screens, I could see the disappearing car. The deer had been tossed hastily across the trunk and there were antlers profiled to the right. Pig? Brother? I could not bear to sit and think, so I walked to the summer-house gate, left open by the hunters. I started to go through but saw drops of blood at my feet. I closed the gate and turned away, to walk back to the log cabin by way of the road. I did not want to see the blood soaking into our green pastures.

After I had drunk the remainder of the breakfast coffee and got over the jitters, which always come on me after danger has passed, I managed to give Ade a reasonably coherent account of my half-hour walk.

"Speculation won't help," Ade said, closing the door.

"We don't own the deer, of course," he said, "but this shooting around the house is deadly dangerous."

"I don't think there'll be any more this season," I said, fervently hoping that I would prove to be right. "Mama was always shy of strangers and she's old enough to know what gunshots mean. The other deer were never frightened before in their lives, by people that is. We made them vulnerable."

"Yes, but I'll bet the ones that are left are heading for far places right now." He looked out at the grain in the yard. "D'you think they'll come back?"

"Some of them will," I answered, and refused to think of which ones or how many. The picture of them resting in the yard the evening before was very clear to me and I knew that the peace and security that had been ours, and our wild friends', too, would not be the same again.

Ade put out grain as usual that night. In the morning a light snow covered the ground but the only tracks were those of a snowshoe hare and some mice. As I was looking at the barely touched grain, a gray jay warbled sweetly from a branch. I held out a piece of bread and the bird dropped to my hand. The feathers around its beak were red with the blood of a deer it had been feeding on. As it flew away and I looked at the scarlet dots left on my fingers, I wondered who would never again lie in the yard, contentedly chewing a cud. Starface, so young that he still had spots only a few weeks earlier? Mama, or the daughters she had reared so devotedly? Pig, with his fine rack and his snorty, touchy temper? I shall never learn whose blood came back to my hand, but I know that some essence of the dead stays with me in the soaring birds and their descendants. Such is the continuity of life.

Two nights after the season closed I heard the bleating outside. It came and went, came and went, like the crying of a lamb, lost and running in panic. It was a fawn, but whether one of Mama's or a stranger I could not tell, because it fled into the brush if I so much as cracked the door. Finally Ade went out and found its tracks in the snow around a place at the edge of the forest where we sometimes fed our deer. Hoping that it was one we knew and that fresh food in a familiar place might help it, he put out mixed grain and we stayed inside, curtains drawn so that our movements might not alarm it. But all night the pitiful bleating went on.

In the morning Starface was lying near the untouched food. When I stepped outside, he jumped up, shivering and bleating, and leaped into the forest, where we could see him watching us.

"He's had a bad fright," I said, "but this is his home, in spite of humans being here. He was born and reared here, so he's come back to wait for Mama."

"What d'you think we ought to do?" Ade asked.

"Keep plenty of food there. Stay inside as much as we can. Hope he'll quiet down and eat. If Mama doesn't come back—" I swallowed, then said firmly, "soon, he'll be in bad shape from malnutrition. Starvation's probably the better word."

But he would not eat, even though I took him oatmeal and Ade cut the tenderest cedar for him. He finally drank a little warm milk that I took out in a bowl.

Day and night he walked up and down in the clearing, listening and bleating, now and then leaping eagerly forward at some sound, only to come back, head hanging, and lie down. After four days of this, he no longer leaped away from us, but lay still, only lifting his head unless we came too close, when he would get up with an effort and walk away a short distance. Occasionally he stood up and gave his bleating call, then lay back down as though he had no strength left to call for a mother who did not answer.

Ade and I were both eating with an effort and losing sleep as we watched and waited with him.

"He can't be that starved," Ade said. "There's plenty of fat on him. There ought to be something we can do."

"No. He's plenty big enough to look after himself, and he would if he hadn't suffered some severe shock. He's dying of loneliness and fear. He hasn't any of the bred-in tameness of a lost puppy. He's a wild animal—and right now we are the enemy."

I walked to the west window and looked sadly into the woods where Starface and Little Buck had had such carefree romps during the summer—and, high on the hill, I saw a deer moving slowly and cautiously through the brush.

"Hey," Ade called. "He's standing up. He hears something."

Together we watched Pretty limp into the yard. Starface backed away when he caught her scent, but kept his head forward and his ears cocked. She glanced at him, then settled to eat, blood trickling from an unhealed bullet wound in her right hind quarter.

"She's not seriously hurt, I think," Ade said. "She's been hit running away and the bullet's lodged in a muscle.

She couldn't walk so well, maybe not at all, if a bone were broken or a tendon cut. It'll probably just heal over."

"Look at Starface," I said.

Inch by inch, quivering as if with uncertainty and eagerness, neck stretching forward, he was approaching Pretty. I remembered that he had known her for only a couple of weeks before the shooting scattered the group. He would probably have run right up to Fuzzy—but I didn't think any of us would see Fuzzy again. She had ambled up to the wrong human, else she would surely have come back before this.

Pretty paid no attention to Starface until he was almost within touching distance. Then she looked up and turned her ears toward him. They stood so for perhaps three minutes. Then she stretched her head forward and Starface reached out, to receive a lick on his black nosetip. Though Pretty as yet had no fawns of her own, she showed us that she knew how to take care of one as well as any experienced doe. While Starface stood close to her, she turned her head to lick his face and eyelashes clean, then nudged him around so that she could lick behind his ears. He leaned against her side for a moment, then bent his head and began to clean up the oatmeal. Clearly, being adopted made all the difference in the world.

It seemed strange to see only two deer in the yard. I missed Fuzzy's friendly ways and found myself watching the brush for Pig and Brother, although I knew one was dead and felt sure the sound that had waked me on the first morning of the open season had signaled the shooting of the other. I still hoped that Mama might have escaped, although Starface's solitary arrival made this doubtful.

Mama would not leave her fawns if she could help it. But if she had run for her life, Starface might have been so frightened that he ran away from her and could find his home place but not his mother. Ade believed she was alive, but staying in hiding out of caution. Neither of us mentioned Peter.

On the second of December we had a snowstorm that blanketed the earth and bent the trees. In the midst of it we heard a deer blowing—once, again, and then a muffled stomp. We almost knocked each other down getting the door open. There, under Peter's tree, was Mama, striking furiously at a hare who had presumed to come for some grain and salt. There was no sign of Little Buck. Someone had shot him, and Mama, threatening and checking our scent, was now as cautious as she had been when Peter first introduced her to our yard.

She forgot the hare when Starface came running to her from the brush. She licked him on whatever part he displayed near her face as he bounced and leaped and curvetted around her. He pounded her with his front hoofs and ran in wild circles, while she turned this way and that, trying to keep him in view. He bounded to meet Pretty, who was making her beautiful, quiet entrance, jumped up and bumped her face with his head, whirled to sidle against Mama with such force that she had to sidestep to balance herself. Then he stood quietly, rubbing his chin on the back of her neck, while she curved her head around to nose his side.

December 3 to January 27

Swaying white curtains of snow blotted out the forest again next morning. The temperature dropped slowly from the high twenties to below zero and a whining wind began to clear the heavy load from the trees and pack the fine, shiny particles. When the storm passed on the fifth of December, we were as isolated as though we were on an island where high waves hammered the shore. The lake was closed with ice too thin for walking. The road would be hard to travel even on snowshoes because snow hollows alternated with high drifts, some as tall as I am, their tops undercut and unstable. Travel through the woods, not easy at any time, would try the strength and experience of an Indian.

Isolation like this, which our pioneering forefathers took for granted, can disrupt common sense. There is no greater chance that you will develop acute appendicitis than at any other time, but some perverseness of mind makes it *seem* more likely to happen. If you let this kind of thinking run wild, the warm, safe cabin can become a trap, menaced by trees about to fall and stoves about to overheat and burn down your shelter. Your anxiety makes you accident-prone and then you are faced with real danger: yourself out of control.

During our first winter here I had some moments when I started to give way to this feeling of helplessness, but watching the birds quickly cured me. Although they were not shut in, the food on which their lives depended might be frozen or buried out of reach. Not handicapped by the human capacity for worry, they went about their affairs, making special efforts. It came to me that security which depends on something outside of yourself is one of the great modern illusions, that such security as an individual may have comes from a recognition of his abilities and limitations, along with self-confidence and a willingness to face and make the best of uncontrollable happenings. Life in isolation would be unbearable, indeed impossible, under other conditions.

While Ade shoveled our paths, I watched Mama, Pretty, and Starface patiently opening their trails. First of all, Mama shoved her way up our path to the road, as though to see whether it was closed to the outside. Then she led the other two back and forth over the paths they had used in summer, making every little turn and curve as though they were marked. I still wonder how she so accurately followed these paths. Perhaps lingering scent reached her through the snow. While they walked, the deer browsed on the maple, catching it in their mouths and breaking it down to get at the twigs. After they had cleared enough trails in our yard, they headed across the road to open their way deeper into the woods.

During the two days when the snow closed the road, the deer were as free of fear as they had been before the hunting. Even though Mama had lost four of her six children and Pretty's wounded leg was still stiff, they seemed to know that no harm had come to them, or would come, from Ade and me. Then we heard the distant rumble and clank of the snowplow, sounds as familiar to the deer as to us. Mama stood guard while the other two hastily ate, then she exchanged places with Pretty to lick up a few mouthfuls herself. Before the plow reached us, the deer had quietly faded out of sight.

"I was getting a little worried," Ade said, as we watched the red and green, yellow and white lights of the plow flash through the brush. "I thought the deer had got over their fright, but Mama knows her way around. Those three aren't going to have anything to do with strangers in the future."

The deer stayed away two days, perhaps to make sure the intruding monster had gone. They had no sooner run across the yard to the much wanted grain than Pretty struck at Mama, and reared up, grunting and ready to fight for both food and the top position in the family. Mama snorted and reared, almost a head shorter than Pretty. Starface backed up, staring. Ade said "Nuts!" and walked out to put two more piles of grain in well-separated positions. Mama did not give ground. Pretty looked at the grain, sagged gracefully to all four feet, and went quietly away to eat. Just to show who was boss, I think, Mama chased her away twice; then, with the domestic situation settled, they finished their meal.

Starface was a strong, lively fawn, with a coat so furry and thick that it looked as though it had been brushed the wrong way. He seemed to miss Little Buck, listening and looking into the brush as he had looked for Mama, perhaps thinking that his brother might come back, too. Sometimes he practiced fighting by himself, lowering his head and shoving dispiritedly at a stump. Mama and Pretty were watching this one afternoon, when the does' ears lifted and they thrust their heads forward, moving from side to side in a most excited manner.

At the edge of the forest stood Peter. Antlered and unharmed, our beloved gentle buck had come back.

Ade began to grind carrots. I peeled some potatoes I did not need so that Peter might have the skins, and recklessly gave my last bit of lettuce to make his homecoming dinner a bit festive.

"He's getting old, isn't he?" I asked, as we watched him eat.

"I think so. His antlers aren't quite as heavy as last year and he moves as if he were a little tired or stiff. But maybe I imagine that."

"No, you don't. From the way his antlers are deteriorating I'd guess he was coming up to eleven, maybe twelve years next spring," I said. "He might be older than that."

"He's lasted this long because he's wary, and we fed him," Ade said. "There were strangers around here early last fall, just looking at the colors. I think that's why he didn't come back in October. And I'll bet he took off at the first shot, if he was near enough to hear it. He has the wisdom of his years. That's what accumulated experience can add up to."

Peter finished his meal and stood chewing his cud, watching Starface, who was again fighting his one-sided battle with the stump. I was thinking that it would give him very strong neck and shoulder muscles, when he looked at Peter and started as though he had not seen him come into the yard. Then he approached the big buck slowly and with great caution, perhaps remembering that Pig, not nearly so powerful, had given him a lively reception. Peter did not move. Starface came up in front of him and lowered his fuzzy head. Peter backed up a step and bent down, very carefully adjusting his antlered head against Starface's; he spread his front feet as though bracing himself and waited. Starface shoved mightily and Peter gave ground for one step, but Ade and I could see that his muscles were relaxed. Then he pushed forward easily, until Starface, braced and resisting with all his young strength, was forced back three steps. Peter then stood perfectly still while Starface withdrew his head from the dangerous spikes encircling it.

Starface pranced and shook his ears, frisked around the clearing, then came back to lower his head again to Peter, who had resumed his cud-chewing. This time Peter stepped away from the lower cedar branches and reared straight up on his hind feet. Any adult whitetail in this position is taller than most men, and Peter, with his antlers adding more than a foot to his already considerable height, was spectacular. Starface, after two stumbling attempts, stood up to face him, the top of his head not reaching to the other's jaw. Soon he could balance and stand almost as

easily as Peter. Then Peter turned to the side, away from Starface, and gave a demonstration of pawing and striking, his front hoofs slashing the air too fast for my eye to follow. After Starface had attempted this, Peter reared again to strike with both front feet at once, dropping forward at the same time and delivering a very heavy blow to his non-existent adversary.

Starface learned rapidly and all went well until Peter dropped both antlers somewhere in the woods and stopped the fighting practice while his pedicels healed. Then Starface decided to put his techniques into practice, choosing Mama for his opponent, perhaps because she was small, perhaps because as his mother she might be most long-suffering. He reared and snorted and struck at her when she was trying to eat until she had enough. As his sharp little hoofs descended on her bent neck, she reared, whirled, and struck so rapidly and expertly that he scuttled away in confusion. From then on he practiced by attacking a cedar trunk, whose bark still bears scars made by his flashing hoofs.

By the first of the year, the deer had settled into quiet ways. They roamed all day and ambled in at dusk, much as cows return to their barnyard. They crunched their corn and nibbled the cedar Ade was cutting again, because the dry summer had spoiled the seed crop and the squirrels were not dropping bits of cedar through the woods as they cut cones. Peter chewed his cud under his tree. Mama and Pretty, with Starface who was growing more like Peter every day, rested and chewed cud on the bank.

Pretty's wound had healed without a trace, but she bolted at any sudden loud noise. Mama and Peter accepted most noises, but once when a freezing tree burst with a sound like a rifle shot, the deer were all gone in a flash. When ice fishermen were in the area and cars moved on the road, we did not see the deer and put out grain, which they came to eat in the dead of night. We were glad to see that they had adapted to the dangers which outsiders might bring, but regretted that neither Mama nor Pretty were likely to bear fawns here in the future.

Near the end of January the deer became very restless, stomping, listening, testing the air as they did when strong wind noises covered the other sounds of the forest. Not one, but two guards stood watch at all times and Starface was quickly herded back to the others if he started to browse into the woods.

Then, on a Friday morning, although the lake thronged with ice fishermen, the deer came into the yard and stayed all day. They paid no attention to the voices from the lake and kept their ears and noses turned toward the woods and the road. They slept in the clearing that night, their beds in the snow close together as though for protection, and, while the others rested, the two changing guards kept watch.

In the morning it was thirty below zero and was lightly snowing, with a steady wind packing the new fall smooth and hard. The deer stood in a group under Peter's tree, ignoring the birds and squirrels that squabbled in the corn around their feet. When Ade left at a quarter to eleven to get the Saturday mail, the wind was slacking and the snow had stopped, but the deer stayed where they were, backs and heads plastered with white.

The mail arrived at the juncture of our road with the main trail at a quarter to twelve. Allowing a few minutes extra for the mailman's arrival, Ade should have been back by one at the latest. But he had not returned by two thirty. The sky had not cleared and the temperature had risen little without the direct sun. It was unlikely that anything was wrong, but should he slip and fall, sprain an ankle or snap a bone, he could quite literally freeze before someone happened along to help. I waited until three o'clock, figuring that it would be turning dark at four thirty and I would have enough time to walk to the end of the side road and back before then. I put on my boots and my padded jacket, pulled a knitted cap down over my ears and mittens onto my hands, stuffed a parcel of cookies into a pocket, and set out to meet Ade.

The road rose and fell, wound and turned, before me. The starchy snow creaked and snapped under my feet. I slid down steep little hills and puffed up others, without seeing a sign of life except Ade's tracks leading ahead. The high snowbanks, accumulations from the earlier plowing, were backed by walls of trees, their boughs reaching toward each other, almost touching above my head. I was walking through a white-paved, black-and-white-walled crevasse, where every quiet vista revealed by the twisting of the road was more beautiful than the last, with a faraway patch of pale blue, where the sky was clearing in the west, as my goal. I was so lost in my feeling of solitude that I did not know Ade had topped a hill ahead until he hailed me.

We met with a kind of surprise, as though we were strangers coming on each other somewhere in the Arctic wastes.

"I hope you weren't worried," he said. "They had a lot more snow toward town and the mail had to wait until it could follow the plow."

"I came on just in case. It's queer, isn't it? Nothing moving anywhere. The cold, I suppose."

"Could be. But there *is* something moving. Care to walk on another half mile?"

He dropped his heavy packsack of mail beside the road and accepted cookies from the parcel I had brought. Munching, we went back over the tracks he had just made. On the top of a hill I looked down at the footprints of a timber wolf.

"He's a giant," I said. "His forepaws must be bigger than my hands!"

"He was here when I walked out this morning," Ade said. "I saw him from the last hill we came over. He saw me at the same time and turned off into the woods. See the tracks? He looked as big as a Great Dane."

"He's headed toward the cabin," I said. "Probably he passed me as I walked this way." I turned around and started back. "He's after the deer. They knew he was around."

"No need to trot yourself out of breath. It's too cold to overstrain. If he kept straight on he's reached our place a long time ago. The deer are downwind. They'll have moved out ahead of him."

When we reached the cabin, the deer were gone. Their feed was untouched next morning and during the night tracks showed where the wolf had walked down our path and crisscrossed the yard before going away to the east.

"Maybe we ought to follow his tracks," I said. "He'll run from man scent if it's coming toward him."

"Better not, I think. If the deer are hiding out anywhere close by they might be more disturbed if we suddenly appear in some place that has always been deer-only country. They had their experience with people in the woods last fall."

"Yes. It'd be interesting to know how they'd react to us out there now, but they've enough to watch out for without us."

Ade made a special short trip for cedar and I kept the grain piles renewed after the onslaughts of the jays and squirrels.

And we waited.

On Tuesday afternoon we sighed with relief as Mama stepped from the brush with Pretty and Starface close behind. They did not seem nervous, so we assumed that the wolf had gone on, but they watched their trails. And so did we, for Peter. But he did not come that night, nor the next, nor the next.

On Friday morning Ade came in after getting oil and found me staring out of the window.

"All you've done the last few days is look out the window and wonder what's happened to Peter," he said gently. "I went on up to the road just now. There're tracks—plain ones. What d'you say we go see what we can see before some fishermen come in and their tire tracks wreck the trail?"

I welcomed the idea of action.

"It's possible he might be hurt," I said, yanking up the zipper on my jacket. "There are wolf traps set around here, and if they aren't set right, they can catch deer. He might let us get close enough to help, don't you think?"

"Well—he might. Come on. Let's go."

I stopped to get my breath after the steep climb through the deep snow of the path, and stared at the still-sharp marks of the wolf's feet on the road. I shivered.

"He's a big one, all right," Ade said.

We moved eastward along the line of loping foot marks.

"I wonder how big," I said, trying to make conversation, but Ade, just ahead, was looking into the woods that lay between the road and the lake. The line of wolf tracks turned off along a deer trail.

We followed easily because the deer had avoided this trail since the wolf's use of it and the tracks were uncluttered. Soon we came to one small and two moderately large hollows in the snow, where Starface, Mama, and Pretty had been sleeping, and from which they had sprung away ahead of the wolf.

"They must have circled around after they left the clearing and made these beds Saturday sometime," Ade guessed. "The wind was from the northwest and the wolf followed the road just south of their trail. Downwind of them so they couldn't smell him. He must have got almighty close before they ran."

We lost the trail in thick brush, floundered through deep snow, found a wolf track and confused deer tracks in the thin snow of a protected spot, and finally came out on the road again through a fresh break in the edging snow bank. The small heart-shaped marks of Starface's hoofs led east, with the big tracks of the running wolf sometimes superimposed, so that we knew he was following.

"The wolf cut him off from the others," Ade said.

"However did he get away? It's silly to think he could outrun such a powerful, fast animal!"

Ade shook his head and we walked on. Even though I knew that Starface was safe, I began to be sorry I had come. I lagged behind, wanting to say, "Let's go home," in spite of knowing that it would be best to read what we could of the story.

Suddenly Ade stopped, looked up the hill on the south side of the road, then downhill on its other side into the woods near the shore.

"That's Peter's track," he said, a little too calmly, and my uneasiness clotted into ice in the pit of my stomach.

The mark of Peter's dented front hoof was plain. His tracks came from the south, crossed the road, and continued on to the north. Ahead of us, the trail of the leaping fawn was still clear—but the wolf tracks no longer followed it. They turned north on Peter's trail. I started to follow them, but Ade pulled me back.

"It's no use," he said, and I think that he, as well as I, had known that from the start. "Peter was big and strong and he could lead the wolf for miles."

He did not add that Peter was old and that the tracks were headed for the lake ice. Nor did he say that neither of us would want to find what probably lay at the end of that trail, no matter how long or short it might be.

"But what chance brought Peter here, right in front of the wolf?" I asked.

Ade pointed to the tracks. Peter had run straight toward the wolf and Starface.

"He was running into the wind," he said. "He should have smelled both of them. I think he came to help Starface—and he was successful."

I looked numbly at the story in the snow, tried to speak, and could not. Ade touched my shoulder and turned me toward home.

"Remember how he came to quiet Snowboots when the wolves killed his twin? And how he stood aside and let Pig and Brother eat all his cedar when they were small and hungry? Starface is small and he needed help, too." Ade looked into the shadows, where the tracks were lost. "Peter was brave and gentle—and generous. He not only shared, he gave."

epilogue

THE GIFT

Years have passed since the wolf followed Peter away from Starface, but I still remember watching, waiting, hoping a little that the long road he had taken might have had a turning somewhere, but he did not return. One night a month after he had gone I thought I heard a tap on the step and slipped out of bed to look just once more.

The night was very cold, with the branches stirring slightly in a silent breeze. The moonlight poured across the open spaces in silver rivers and fell in pale, glimmering splotches between the branches. I looked at the hollow that Peter had dug in the snow as he licked to get every taste of salt fallen from his grain. I looked at the place under the cedar tree where he had stood to chew his cud in comfort and in safety. The moon shadows moved and I could almost see him there. Then, from far away, the wild and beautiful howl of a wolf came to my ears.

The shadows under the tree were only shadows. I knew that Peter would not come again. But he was not lost to us. I could never be sure what had happened to him—you never can be when a wild creature goes back to its own world—but I felt that he still lived in the wolves on the hills, in the ravens and gray jays and foxes, in the soil their droppings fertilize, in the green things that grow there, in the waters that quench the thirst of the earth. Life and death rise, one from the other, as day follows night. Nothing can be lost, for nothing exists alone.

When Peter came into our yard, we had a choice to make. We could stand by and see for ourselves how a deer starved to death. We could assume that he had no chance of recovery and kill him, in the way called humane. Or we could reach out with the compassion that has the power to lift man above the brute level. We chose the last, and when Ade cut the first cedar branch for Peter, he stirred the air among the branches. This whisper of a breeze turned into a wide-spreading wind, swaying the trees and changing the life of the forest. And it still reaches out and blows back to us, sometimes a raging, violent gale, more often a soft and gentle zephyr.

Mama is still here, a matriarch, wary, wise, a firm disciplinarian in spite of her years, for she is very old. Her back is deeply swayed. The skin of her haunches fits loosely over muscles sharply defined and no longer gracefully padded with fat. Her teeth are so worn down that her cheeks wrinkle out when she chews. The skin sags on her belly where once her udder swelled, and she bears fawns no longer. Her work is almost done.

Last winter was a long and bitter one, with snow piling deep, deep near its end. And out of the forest, from the hills and the cutover lands and the swamps, where the snow locked the browse away, came the deer—Mama's children, and Peter's, back to the place where they had wintered as fawns. They brought their children and their children's children, and strangers followed timidly.

Among them were two thin, motherless, golden-brown fawns, so weak that they lacked spirit and did not dare approach the grain. Pretty, as she had once cared for Starface, adopted the little doe, whose face was as innocent and lovely as an opening rose, and Starface, sleek and handsome in his maturity, hooked a foreleg across the little buck's shoulders and gave him a shove that sent him stumbling in to eat. One night I heard grunting near our south window and looked out to see Snowboots, a white-stockinged forest king as impressive as Peter, standing where the cedar garden once had been, perhaps dimly remembering that he had smelled cedar there years before. And Mama was always busy—licking behind young ears, keeping order around the grain piles, mothering all of them, down to her great-great-great-grandchildren.

They dug through the snow with their hoofs to get at mosses and hidden plants; they wandered to lick up the cedar the squirrels and the wind had brought down; they milled in the yard and shoved to get at the life-giving grain. They trampled the snow under the trees into a playground where the fawns leaped and chased each other, flung up their heels and whirled and twisted, while the does stood quietly watching and the bucks were only shadows behind the clustered stems of the brush. Then, with the rising of the sap and the melting of the snow, they went away as gently as mist on a sunny morning.

Tonight, as another year nears its end, it is very quiet. An hour ago I stood under a sky of infinite blackness, abounding in stars. I had not known they could fill the sky in such numbers, that they could shine like that—diamond-bright, even their colors clear through the clean, dry air. Slowly the light of the rising moon spread above the trees, to blend with the Milky Way and hide the lesser stars, but still the nearer and greater suns blazed behind the shimmering veil of frost.

I watched Orion, tall as Creation, crossing the sky with strides light-years long, wearing red Betelgeuse for an epaulet and blue-white Rigel for a shoe buckle. I slipped to a knee on the path and my out-thrust hand went through the snow to the frozen earth. Years before I had watched Orion from a city window, with my hand on the aluminum and concrete of its sill—the same transformed stardust as the crumbled granite of our soil.

Moonlight flooded between the trees as it had on the night when I last looked for Peter, and gliding in and out of tonight's moonstreams were Mama, Pretty and her latest fawns, and Starface in antlered majesty. I thought of cities and forests, of man and his brothers in fur, of the stars—and of Peter. I felt the snow melting on my hand and knew that to touch a snowflake, to feed Peter, was to touch them all.

If we had not brought Peter back from the edge of death, he would not have led Mama to stay with us. Starface would not have been born. Most of the things—the personal things—I have been writing about would never have happened. And the wind from the branches Ade moved is still blowing. When these deer have gone on the long road that Peter, and so many others, have taken, there will be deer still, following the old trails through the forest,

perhaps to come to us for help in another winter of bitter cold and deep snow.

Peter brought them to us, he left them for us, a gift priceless beyond all accounting. What can I say of him?

He was Peter, our buck with the generous heart.

A Note About the Author

Helen Hoover was born in 1910 in Greenfield, Ohio, and attended Ohio University where she studied chemistry and physics. Before she and her artist-husband moved to their present home on the Minnesota-Canadian border, Mrs. Hoover worked in Chicago as a chemist and as research metallurgist, in the latter capacity with the International Harvester Company from 1948 to 1954. In 1959 Mrs. Hoover received the Annual Achievement Award of the Metal Treating Institute. On several occasions during this period she enrolled in courses in biology at the University of Chicago. Since 1954 Mrs. Hoover has been a contributor to many nature magazines and is the author of *The Long Shadowed Forest*, published in 1963, *A Place in the Woods* (1969), and *The Years of the Forest* (1973).

A Note on the Type

The text of this book was set on the Linotype in Janson,
a recutting made direct from type cast from matrices
long thought to have been made by the Dutchman
Anton Janson, who was a practicing type founder in
Leipzig during the years 1668–87. However it has been
conclusively demonstrated that these types are actually
the work of Nicholas Kis (1650–1702), a Hungarian who
most probably learned his trade from the master Dutch
type founder Kirk Voskens. The type is an excellent
example of the influential and sturdy Dutch types that
prevailed in England up to the time William Caslon
developed his own incomparable designs from these
Dutch faces.

The book was composed by Brown Bros. Linotypers, Inc.,
New York, printed and bound by
The Haddon Craftsmen, Inc., Scranton, Penn.